Plowboys, Cowboys and Slanted Pigs

A COLLECTION BY JERRY FLEMMONS

WITH A FOREWORD BY GEORGE DOLAN
DRAWINGS BY J. D. CROWE

D1707050

Texas Christian University Press
Fort Worth, Texas

Library of Congress Cataloging in Publication Data
Flemmons, Jerry.
  Plowboys, cowboys, and slanted pigs.
  I. Title.
PN4874.F513A25 1984   814'.54   84-2421
ISBN 0-912646-90-X
ISBN 0-912646-95-0 (pbk.)

Designed by Whitehead & Whitehead/Austin

PLOWBOYS, COWBOYS AND SLANTED PIGS

CONTENTS

FOREWORD   *ix*

PREFACE   *xiii*

ON, YE PLOWBOYS!   *1*

MY GIFT TO AMERICA   *11*

JFK—TWENTY YEARS AFTER   *15*

THOSE AWFUL GOOD OLE DAYS   *19*

ANDROS: 'FANTASY ISLAND' WITH A HOT TUB   *25*

TRAGEDY IN WISE COUNTY   *33*

THE YEAR THAT COST US DEAR   *43*

THE BEST MAN EVER WORN OUT BY A NEWSPAPER   *45*

COWBOYS   *55*

THE SCREWDRIVER AND OTHER DANGEROUS WEAPONS   *71*

SMITING A SINFUL WORLD   *75*

THE LOST ART OF TORTILLA ROLLING   *91*

COWTOWN CULTURE   *95*

TEXAS CUISINE   *103*

AMERICA'S BEST TOURIST TRAP   *111*

A SLANTED PIG CHRISTMAS   *115*

PASSING   *121*

FAVORITE TEXAS WORDS   *125*

EAST TEXAS   *129*

BAH! ON BASEBALL   *137*

WHEN A PUN'S SPUN   *141*

FOR LORD BYRON NELSON, STILL THE MUSIC
   LINGERS   *145*

EL PASO   *153*

PALM SPRINGS: GILT, GLIT AND GRIT   *159*

FOURTH OF JULY   *169*

A PLAGUE OF TIPPING   *173*

CITY OF HISTORY, RIVER OF GRACE   *179*

TEXANS IN NEW YORK   *189*

THE FORT WORTH STRANGERS   *205*

AFTER THE FACT   *219*

A CHRISTMAS STORY   *223*

FOREWORD

This Flemmons sampler—a selection of Jerry Flemmons' writings during a 20-year period—reveals his exquisitely deft touch with humor, pathos, drama.

These selections aren't necessarily his best, nor are they especially his favorites. They're among those that he liked well enough to clip and toss into a box. The TCU Press chose from among those.

If Jerry had tossed cuttings of *all* his articles worthy of inclusion, he'd have needed a box capable of accommodating the carcass of a Great White Whale.

Those of us who have been closely associated with Jerry during those 20 years still shake our heads in wonder at the prose that flows from his typewriter. It has so much more style and grace—and this is meant in the kindliest way—than *he.*

This incongruity is as astonishing as dining at one of Jerry's favorite eating places (some chicken-fried steak joint), ordering a glass of house wine and seeing the waiter pour from a dusty, cobwebby bottle of Lafite Rothschild.

Jerry, despite all the acclaim he has received, has never lost the common touch. He couldn't if he tried.

He goes around looking more like a warehouse shipping clerk than a newspaperman-author who has lived it up in more than a hundred countries. A friend says: "He hasn't let success go to his *wardrobe.*"

If he's going to some nice place for lunch, he'll pull a corduroy jacket over his wash-n-wear shirt, unbuttoned at the collar, and wipe his boot toes on the backs of his khaki pantslegs. You'd have to throw him down and hold him to get a necktie around his throat. He owns *one,* a brown-striped four-in-hand with matching enchilada stains.

I'm told that when he checked out a few purchases one day at a Safeway Store the clerk asked him for food stamps.

Embarrassing things of one sort or another are always happening to Jerry. He's a shy, sensitive creature who embarrasses easily.

I took him to Ridglea Country Club one day for a round of golf and we found several foursomes waiting at the first tee. The starter told us to play the back nine first.

"Did you get a good look at the starter?" I asked, as we trudged to the 10th tee. "That guy intimidates me. He looks like a British Army major, with that red face, bristly mustache and patronizing manner, just back from 20 years of showing the natives who's boss in Inja. He stands there at parade rest, *watching*, as you hit your first tee shot of the day. I've *never* hit a decent drive with him watching."

Jerry was in good form that day. His backswing, so deliberate you could time a soft-boiled egg by it, never wavered, nor did it wobble. Every tee shot on that back nine was long and true.

When we reached the No. 1 tee, after playing those nine holes, it was his honor. He had won the ninth hole. To be honest, he had won the other eight, too.

We were the only golfers at the No. 1 tee, so the major was able to give Jerry his undivided attention. Jerry felt the major's critical eye on him as he started that slow, slow backswing. Jerry's driver wavered. And wobbled. The clubhead struck the ball a glancing blow, sending it bouncing 20 yards in front of the tee. The major executed a contemptuous about-face. Jerry's face flamed.

He grimly took out his No. 2 wood, marched to his ball, swung lustily and the ball screamed low and long down the middle of the fairway. Jerry looked back quickly to make sure the major had seen *that* shot. The major still had his back turned.

Going places with Jerry is stimulating. Such unforgettable moments often occur. For he also is bad-service prone.

He goes through life quietly but determinedly demanding to see the manager.

An adversary relationship develops the moment a waitress hands him a menu. Each seems to realize instinctively that the other is a natural enemy. It's the same mutual revelation that a dog and cat experience when they meet. Jerry adamantly refuses to tip for below-average service. You'd be amazed at how little he spends on tips, because below-average service is about all he ever gets.

But his problems with service aren't restricted to restaurants. Things, for him, go awry in all sorts of places. Once, in Florida, he had booked an early-morning flight to Texas.

The hotel operator forgot his wake-up call. Jerry awoke just in time to pack and get to the limousine on time. No shower, no shave, no breakfast.

Then the limo driver was 30 minutes late.

When Jerry's clothes on hangers were stashed in the limo, one hanger slipped and the hook ripped the front of a new shirt. Then, when his bag was unloaded and placed by the curb at the airport, a car ran over it.

Next, the airline ticket clerk waited on someone else when it was Jerry's turn. Jerry explained the error to the clerk in a low tone, through clenched teeth.

After the plane landed at Love Field in Dallas, Jerry took his coat from the overhead rack and an oxygen bottle came down with it, splitting the bridge of his nose.

Let it be said, to his everlasting credit, that Jerry, no matter how provoking the circumstances, never stomps or hollers or throws things. He just *seethes*.

Such stoicism must be hereditary. So must Jerry's work ethic. He mentions, in this collection, his grandfather's scratching out a living on a small farm. Grandpa excelled at his craft, as Jerry does at his. Grandpa won the respect of his neighbors, as Jerry has of his colleagues and competitors.

A neighbor paid this tribute to Grandpa's skill: "Hilman shore keeps his cotton weeded good."

If that neighbor were alive today, and if he knew Jerry's work as columnist, travel editor, magazine writer, author and playwright, I'll bet he'd say, every bit as admiringly: "That peckerwood shore kin shovel it."

George Dolan

PREFACE

As a journalist for more than twenty years, Jerry Flemmons has covered major international stories—the Kennedy assassination, the shootings from the University of Texas tower. In 1968, he was named travel editor for the *Fort Worth Star-Telegram*, and from 1968 until 1974 he was also a columnist for the paper. In the mid-1970s, he took two leaves of absence to research and write *Amon*, the life story of Amon G. Carter, founder of the *Star-Telegram*. Today, Jerry is still travel editor and works on special projects such as the section of reminiscences published on the twentieth anniversary of the assassination of John Fitzgerald Kennedy. This book is a sampling of Jerry's writing—travel pieces, selections from the six-year period he was a general columnist, passages from the books *Amon* and *Texas*, magazine articles from *Vision*, *Vista*, *Ford Times* and *Southern Living*.

FOR MY MOTHER

1968

ON, YE PLOWBOYS!

A long time ago when Plowboys were upon the land they played basketball in Texas, and in the 1930s basketball in Texas was considered unregenerate and wasteful. It was commonly believed to be as sinful as voting for Alf Landon or buying from a Methodist bootlegger.

For Texans there were no other sports than football and, perhaps, river baptism. Football was a hardshell religion worshipped by the devout in great concrete temples. Football, a natural extension of saloon fights, was The Consummate Proof of Manhood. Basketball, often verbally flogged like an orphan home runaway, was a wimpy sport.

I once heard the following exchange between two small town fathers:

"Yore boy playing football?" inquired the first.

"No," the second admitted, timidly. "He's goin' out for basketball."

"Gawdamighty, can't you break him of it?" exclaimed the first, his voice carrying the conviction that basketball players wore lavender shirts and studied interior decorating.

Perhaps that is why the Plowboys became extinct. They played basketball in a land hostile enough to believe that a man properly wore shorts and undershirt only in bed.

The Plowboys of the 1930s are enshrined today only in two places (three, if you check the archives of *Ripley's Believe It or Not*). First, there are the memories and scrapbooks of William Jennings Wisdom, now 80 years old and slowly going blind. Second, there is the Naismith Basketball Hall of Fame in Springfield, Mass.

W. J. Wisdom will tell you, show you, and the Naismith Hall of Fame will document, the fact that the Plowboys won more consecutive basketball games than any college team in history: 111 of 112 games. Between the final game of the 1932 season and midway into 1937, the redoubtable Plowboys built an eighty-six-game winning streak, lost one game by a single point, then added another 25 straight victories before losing again. In the decade between 1930 and 1940, and with Wisdom providing strategy, the Plowboys lost just ten games. During that 1932–37 winning streak, they outscored opponents about three to one—3,547 to 1,650 points.

Truly, the Plowboys were the Brobdingnagians of Basketball. They played anyone who would play them, including House of David teams. They laughed at larger, over-coached teams and at the height of their power and domination, publicly challenged Southwest Conference basketball teams to a showdown. SWC teams politely cleared their throats and refused. The habitat of Plowboys was a singularly placid little institution called John Tarleton Agricultural College, which was a sort of south-forty farm club in the Texas A&M University system. It was a junior college—uncomfortably known as JTAC—in Stephenville, a smallish north central Texas town. It has become a four-year school, Tarleton State University, an alias taken to disguise its agrarian stain. After JTAC assumed full university status, its students, perhaps horrified that any sports team could be named "Plowboys," threw out the unique sobriquet and installed "Texans" as object of school yells.

In the 1930s Stephenville was a pleasant community encircled by peanut patches and the Bosque River which held absolutely no water except for twenty-five minutes each spring when it flooded half the town. It was bounded on the east by a radiator shop ("Don't cuss that rust, bring it to us") and on the west by an experimental chicken farm at which JTAC first supped fame with a White Leghorn hen. The industrious chicken miss was for the better part of one year the world's champion egg layer. She dropped 319 eggs in 344 days but with only 13 days to go (and well into the world's egg-laying lead), she died. According to yellowed newspaper reports, her death was a grisly one. An autopsy proved she died of egg strangulation, which must have hurt like the dickens. In addition to White Leghorns and Plowboys, Stephenville had three picture shows, a square of downtown stores and a Gothic courthouse, the tower of which was occupied by several hundred bats and a guano-fouled four-faced clock.

JTAC was an exceptional junior college with more than 1,000 enrollment and a reputation for academic excellence. Its sports teams, excepting basketball (which nobody cared about), were Texas powerhouses. At JTAC, as everywhere in Texas, football was dictator. Its Plowboy gridiron teams regularly whipped junior college rivals, several four-year schools and, on occasion, a Southwest Conference team caught unaware.

So, into this academic and Plowboy football lair came a square-faced, compact little man with arrow-flint eyes and a secret habit of listening to symphonic music. W. J. Wisdom. He arrived in 1920 as JTAC business manager and head salesman in the college store. Within his background were a short stint of baseball in the Colorado State League and terms as business teacher at Tyler Commercial College and English Department Chairman at Paducah High School. Wisdom briefly coached a girl's basketball team at Paducah but quit after his female center knocked him down three times in a practice session ("She was bigger and stronger than I was," he remembered).

Because of a lean school budget, Wisdom was forced to begin coaching the Plowboy football team. In 1921–22, 1924–28 and 1932–35, his squads compiled an overall record of 68-28-12, a more than respectable .718 winning percentage. Included in this record were victories over Texas A&M and Baylor University varsities.

When the Depression struck Texas in 1930, Wisdom was drafted as Plowboy basketball coach, too. People didn't expect much to come of it, and even Wisdom can't fully explain the success that followed. He never played a single basketball game, neither in high school nor North Texas State University, where he sat as first chair violinist in the school orchestra. Except for that humiliating moment with the girl center

in Paducah, Wisdom—properly—had ignored basketball. He knew only that it was played indoors and was not at all considered by Texans to be a character-building sport. But he had no choice. He was coach, and he prepared for his new job by going to the school library and reading every available book on the sport.

Wisdom maintained he did not intend to build a basketball dynasty at JTAC. He decided that since he was stuck with the job he might as well try to do it right and provide the school with a basketball team comparable to its football squad. And, beginning in 1930 he filled the rickety old campus gym with basketball players, most of whom slept in a spare room behind the clapwood building. His team practiced and practiced. Wisdom read more books. In 1932, JTAC had a team ready to conquer the known Texas basketball world, such as it was.

Recruiting seems to have been the key to Wisdom's success. He sought out hungry boys who were good athletes, and in Depression-filled Texas, hungry boys were legion. Tom Tinker, who later became head basketball coach for the University of Texas at Arlington, was working with a Civilian Conservation Corps crew on a reclamation project near Mesquite when he saw Wisdom striding toward him.

"You play basketball?" Wisdom asked.

"Not much, but I like baseball," answered the lean, tall Tinker.

"I need basketball players at John Tarleton."

"Where?"

"It's a junior college, and we set the best training table in the state."

The proffered meals sold Tinker, and he became a Plowboy star in a sport he cared very little about.

Jude Smith recalls that Wisdom came to Lamesa and offered him a scholarship to play basketball at JTAC—a generous proposition since Tarleton actually had no athletic scholarships (players were given jobs as janitors and grass mowers to earn tuition and expenses).

But even a job could not help Smith, whose family was

West Texas-poor. "I can't do it, coach," Smith said to Wisdom. "All I've got to my name is one dime."

Wisdom loaned Smith $90 to cover his first year's expenses, and the youngster cut grass and raked leaves for money with which to repay the debt. Jude Smith, whose brother, Preston, would become a Texas governor, was the sparkplug guard during the Plowboys' gravy years.

Joe Headstream, a jolly giant of a center, came off a farm near Ropesville. Owen Spears, a team captain, was a poor boy from Forney, near Dallas. Raymond Blair, Otis Richie and Don Rankin were drafted from nearby Springtown. All became Plowboy stars.

The basketball streak began innocently enough with a 41-39 victory over San Angelo Junior College in the final game of the 1932 season. From that moment on, John Tarleton's agriculture college Plowboys simply demolished everything in their path. They licked every junior college in the state. They humbled four-year colleges like Howard Payne, Abilene Christian, McMurry, Hardin-Simmons, Texas Wesleyan and North Texas State. In five years of play in the Central Texas Conference, the Plowboys lost but a single game, the upset that ended the 86-game winning streak.

JTAC won by heavy-sided margins—92-17, 72-6, 53-4. Rarely was it behind at the half. Expertly coached by Wisdom, the Plowboys averaged fewer than 10 fouls per game during the long siege. They played a waiting game. Wisdom's simple basketball formula was to shoot only when a shot is available, defense man on man, and stay "between your man and the goal and never, never allow a crib shot."

The Plowboys held court in a barn-like gym, bounded on one side by tiered bleachers. Low rafters hampered high shots. When the strain of winning began to show on the Plowboys, Wisdom would urge them to "cut up on the court." Headstream would take blind shots over his head ("He made more than he missed."). Smith and Spears would shoot high and long over the rafters and, in fact, practiced the unusual shot in workout. "We made a lot of them," recalled Smith, who became a high school principal. "Then other teams would attempt the shot, hit the rafters and we would get the ball."

Beating the Plowboys became a cause célèbre. Wisdom said he was challenged by the coach of Texas Wesleyan College, a four-year school. "I didn't want to play them because we had a hard game the next night but I couldn't let them think we were scared," he recalled. "Well, TWC came and they brought nearly all the newspaper sportswriters and photographers in Fort Worth."

"I think they already had their headlines written: 'TWC Ends Plowboy Winning Streak.' That was foolish. In the first eight minutes we were ahead 23-8."

Wisdom suffered with the winning streak. "It was the worst ordeal I have ever been through. There were times when I just could not sleep at night, and I'm sorry to say I often wished we would lose a game just to get out from under the tension," he said.

The record is a remarkable one, if only because JTAC was a junior college and Wisdom had his teams just two years. Twice during the streak he lost his entire starting lineup and had to begin anew. But, said contemporaries, Wisdom had the ability to bring his players to full potential quicker than any other basketball coach in Texas history.

His coaching techniques were low-keyed. He attributed the success to his careful selection of players. "I chose athletes, not basketball players. I gave them freedom to use their natural ability and intuition. I tried to develop their natural tendencies rather than mine," he explained. His pep talks were brief. "I believe you can do it," he would tell players. If the team was behind at the half, he reiterated, "I still believe you can win." And the Plowboys did. Almost to a man, Wisdom's former players claim their coach had a mystical quality. Marshall Hughes, who played during the latter years of the winning streak, said, "I've never in my life seen another man like him. He asked us to play as well as we could and we did. If he said we could beat some team or another, we simply went out and won."

The determination lasted in the players. Almost four decades after the Plowboys' challenge to Southwest Conference teams, Smith declared, "They were afraid we would beat them, and we would have."

When the team was winning heavily, coaches from across America began calling Wisdom, asking for his secret. All he would tell a New England coach was "We just play basketball, that's all there is to it." Possibly there was a little more. His mind seldom was away from the game. He read and devised game plans constantly. He once said he thought the Plowboys were winners because he believed in elimination of errors. To accomplish that, he posted 10 students in the grandstands for each game. Their duty was to watch for and record player errors.

When the end came at the 86th game, it came from the same San Angelo Junior College beaten by JTAC five years earlier to begin the long win column. In mid-1938 the Plowboys climbed into the rattletrap cars they used for road games and drove to San Angelo for a two-game series with the Rams. They won the first game easily enough by 15 points. The next night things began to go wrong.

At halftime the Plowboys were down by three points. Wisdom delivered his I-still-believe-you-can-win speech but it didn't work. San Angelo won the game by a single point, 27-26.

After the loss (which Wisdom professed to welcome), the Plowboys remounted the smoking old cars and rode 150 miles through the night to their home behind the gym. Smith recalled that the players, feeling badly about the loss, came into the gym. Suddenly, the lights came on. The gym was filled by Plowboy supporters, welcoming them home, saying all is forgiven.

The Plowboys won 25 more games before losing again but by then, late 1939, World War II was catching on, the Depression was ending. Hungry boys were becoming Army privates. The Plowboys never again were the same. Wisdom coached until 1943 when he resigned to join the USO. Later he was national secretary of the YMCA, and still later he returned to Stephenville as Chamber of Commerce manager (during this period, he bought a used set of golf clubs, several golfing books, practiced long hours and set a still-existing record—65 for 18 holes—on the city course).

Under Wisdom, Plowboys were god-like and in high demand from senior colleges throughout the country. Smith became the most valuable player at Texas A&M for two consecutive years. Wisdom once watched Texas A&M and the University of Texas play a basketball game. Eight of the 10 starting players were former Plowboys.

Wisdom could have coached at other, larger schools. It was widely reported that in 1937 the University of Texas offered him the head coaching job—if he would bring his five starting Plowboys with him.

But if Wisdom did not accept the jobs, his Plowboys did. Thurman "Slue" Hull and Hughes were Texas University head basketball coaches. Jack Martin was head coach at Lamar Tech, Tinker at UTA.

Lee Williams, executive director of the Naismith Memorial Basketball Hall of Fame, protected the Plowboys' record as college basketball's best. It is a record, Wisdom conceded, that may never be broken.

He looked back on the winning streak with pleasure, because for a little while in north central Texas basketball was something of which to be proud. It almost supplanted football in the minds of Plowboys followers. Not quite, but almost.

Wisdom stopped coaching football in 1935 after his team won nine games, including two victories over senior colleges, and lost one.

A day after the final football game, Wisdom sat down for a cup of coffee in a Stephenville cafe. The loafer at the next stool said, "Too bad about that one game you lost. The football team nearly had a winning season."

Wisdom sputtered and stewed, and from that day on never again coached football. Basketball, and Plowboys, were the winners.

1970

MY GIFT TO AMERICA

Carrying America's economy on my shoulders is a terrible responsibility and I regret that the awesome power has been invested in me. I alone am responsible for the present crisis in the market place. Last January I bought 14 shares of stock in one of our nation's leading firms. The next day, the slump began, continues to this very day, and will endure until I decide to let it up by selling my stock. Realistically, I should have known better. But I thought I would test my control by purchasing a few shares. It still works.

If I wanted, I could bring Wall Street to its knees in a couple of days by investing in something like AT&T. Instantly, AT&T would go into bankruptcy, and the country would be without telephone service, television cables and such. Communications would be at a standstill. The economy would collapse. There would be depression.

I would not do this, of course, but this awful power is there, nevertheless, to use as a club if Wall Street ever should try to cross me.

Early in the 1960s, I discovered I had this talent for causing a stock's value to drop simply by subscribing to a few shares of it when a friend of mine got into the brokerage business.

He urged me to buy a mutual fund because he said mutual funds were great for making my money multiply, and besides, he needed to make a sale. So I purchased $750 of the fund, which included his commission, allowing him to feed his kids that week.

Within days, the mutual fund collapsed, and six months later it had disappeared completely, like some shameful phantom. My friend had all sorts of excuses, none of which seemed plausible.

But we tried again, and he sold me shares in a California television tube factory. Shares were $18 each. A month later there was an announcement that transistors were to be the future of TV sets, and my tube factory shares went to $12, then $9 and finally $1.50.

My broker friend was beginning to suspect me and did not again come around to push stock. I was thinking something was odd, too.

A year or so after the tube firm collapse, I overheard two businessmen raving about a small oil company. It had leases surrounding a huge oil field and simply could not miss striking. It could and did, repeatedly, but only after I bought a few shares.

It was then I recognized my control over Wall Street but vowed never to use it in anger since a lot of little people's jobs depended on me.

Aside from my lapse last January—I truthfully am sorry about that—I have tested this considerable burden only one other time, mostly to make a point to an unbelieving Dallas stock-broker.

Foolishly I told him I could break him financially whenever I pleased and he, equally foolishly, said "Prove it." We devised a test case.

His personal portfolio success was based on the remarkable growth of an airline. On paper, the broker was a millionaire from that stock, which he bought at $28. It had grown to $121. He figured it would go at least to $200.

So, his deal was that he would purchase, in my name, $6,000 of the airline stock. I would receive any profit; he would absorb any loss. That was not a smart deal on his part.

Instantaneously, there was chaos among the airline's management officers. The president was fired. Stock dropped

to $110. New ideas failed. The stock fell to below $100. I urged my friend to sell out. He still had a huge gain. He refused, saying my power was nonexistent in the matter.

Today—this very morning—the airline's stock can be bought for $23 a share. My friend is now a believer.

For those interested, I can offer this market tip. If you want to get in on a good thing, want to buy in just as the market sky-rockets, you should know that I intend next week selling my 14 shares.

It is the least I can do for my country.

1983

JFK–TWENTY YEARS AFTER

*From a special Fort Worth Star-Telegram section of remi-
niscences on the twentieth anniversary of the death of John
Fitzgerald Kennedy.*

Presidents, in what now seem like long ago days, had
a kind of folk-hero quality. To see one up close, in person,
was an event for scrapbooks, snapshots and memories to share
with grandkids.

Teddy Roosevelt came to Fort Worth in 1906 and half of
Tarrant County's 50,000 people cheered him at the railroad
station. Franklin Delano and Eleanor Roosevelt—whose son
Elliott lived in Fort Worth for a while—visited a half-dozen
times, becoming such a familiar sight that a traffic policeman
once shouted to the president: "Hey, Franklin, good to see you
again." Fiesty Harry Truman brought his 1948 re-election
railroad campaign through Fort Worth and later estimated
that "15 acres of people" greeted him.

Presidents always drew a crowd in those days, when they
didn't really seem much different from us. Life in the United
States was not yet tense and mean-spirited. Presidents had not
yet been transposed into impersonal electronic blips, regular
television characters, like Bob Newhart or Fred Flintstone.
They had not yet involved the nation in unwinnable wars and
hadn't been exposed for their participation in dirty tricks.
They had not trained for the White House on the back lots
and sound stages at 20th Century Fox. And their brothers
had not endorsed brands of beer and become a national embarrassment.

It was a time, we are now told, of innocence.

If we had innocence, we have since lost it. And some fix the time, date and place of that loss at 12:30 p.m., Nov. 22, 1963, when shots rang out in Dallas and the youngest man ever to be elected president of the United States slumped over in his convertible.

But that may be far too simplistic a view of the way in which American life has changed.

Twenty years is a short time to live but a long distance to go back. If we had innocence, it was the innocence of an age that appears flash-frozen in the history books, a time seemingly more distant and less innocent than a mere two decades ago.

In November 1963, Jackie Gleason and Ed Sullivan were TV stars. There were Studebakers and Admiration Coffee, Plaid Stamps and Billie Sol Estes. Ward's still was Montgomery Ward's, and *Parade* magazine had decided that it was unseemly for women to ask men for dates. Ford Falcons cost a whopping $1,875. In Texas we were debating liquor-by-the-drink—one anti-drinking *Star-Telegram* reader wrote, "It pleases the communists to know that America spends millions of dollars annually for alcohol that could go toward higher education and missionary work." Texans also had to pay to vote—the $1.75 poll tax. Southwest Conference colleges had agreed to integrate their athletic teams while denying any previous prejudice—after all, the argument went, Southern Methodist University already had performed against a team with black players.

Fort Worth had things now lost to progress and memory: Carlson's Drive-In; the downtown Hollywood, Worth and Palace theaters; Zuider Zee seafood; Hotel Texas; The Farmer's Daughter; Leonard's; George Dolan's hair.

Home mortgages were 4.5 percent for a "6 room frame contemporary, walking distance to Arlington Heights Hi"—$11,000 at $64.50 per month. Experienced secretaries were paid $286 monthly and insurance adjusters, $450. Lavender's Cafeteria served all-you-can-eat dinners for 98 cents, Buddies sold three pounds of hamburger meat for $1, sirloin steak for 79 cents a pound. The *Star-Telegram* cost a nickel.

That November weekend Sears was hiring Santas, the Shrine Circus was in town. TCU was preparing to play Rice in a homecoming game, Bond's had "costly wool dresses" for $10.90, and the Neiman-Marcus Christmas catalog featured his and hers submarines—$18,700 for the pair.

WFAA-TV had scheduled, for the pleasure of its weekend viewers, the movie *The Day the Earth Stood Still.* The theme of the now classic 1950s film was science fiction, or so we believed.

John F. Kennedy: to many ordinary folks he was a hero

As in most things, Fort Worth lagged behind Dallas in extreme political thinking. Being smaller, more taciturn, we had proportionately fewer and less-vocal flakes, and none with any national standing. Our Junior Leaguers never would have spat on LBJ. It was not that some of them did not detest him, but rather because ladies simply did not spit in public.

One squirrely local evangelist, however, actually divined from Holy Scriptures the startling news that John Kennedy was the Antichrist. His reasoning: the president's full name, John Fitzgerald Kennedy, was composed of three words and 21 letters; 3 from 21 is 18; 18 divided by 3 is 6. Three sixes, 666: The Mark of the Beast. You could look it up.

What ordinary Dallas and Fort Worth folks felt about their little nests of zanies is, after two decades, unimportant. Probably they were equally amused and bewildered. What is significant to remember is that they liked and admired John Kennedy. To many of them, as to many others across the country, he would become, perhaps, but only perhaps, the last American hero:

John Fitzgerald Kennedy. 35th and youngest president of the United States. Born May 29, 1917—died Nov. 22, 1963. Oldest surviving son of Joseph and Rose Kennedy. Brother of Robert and Ted, quarterback of the Sunday afternoon Kennedy clan touch football team. He was tall—but in person not as tall as he appeared on television—and toothy, charming, witty, urbane, capable of joking about himself, married to a beautiful woman whose breathless little-girl voice became as recognizable as his Massasschusetts/New England/ nouveau-Irish Boston/Cape Cod accent, which created R's where there were none (Like: "Cuber" for Cuba).

JFK was that rarest of persons, a rich man with a social conscience whose vision bred the Peace Corps, sending thousands of young people into the Third World to teach the hardlearned lessons of America. He hated hats, refused to wear one, and hat sales declined drastically during his brief presidency. He had a bad back, slept only on mattresses braced by hard boards, sat in stiff-backed rocking chairs, one of which was shipped to Fort Worth and placed for his use in Hotel Texas' Suite 850. He was, the supermarket scandal newspapers now tell us, something of a womanizer, a highly successful womanizer.

JFK was uncomfortable with his vice president, Lyndon Johnson, who was pushed on him because of political necessity. However, in what became the closest presidential election in history, it was LBJ who helped the party carry seven Southern states, including Texas. They were a pair: the handsome, sophisticated, Eastern elite JFK and the Hill Country rough, homely LBJ—"like Cary Grant marrying Marjorie Main," someone wrote at the time. But in the end, or rather after the end, it was LBJ who made reality of JFK's vision, who owned the political shrewdness to transport Congress into the New Frontier.

JFK, historians are beginning to realize, was not a very effective president. The Bay of Pigs was a failure, the Cuban missile crisis, at best, a draw. And Congress stonewalled him on very nearly every issue. What JFK brought to the presidency was, if not substance, style. The man had a grand style and an ability to articulate the dream of a world made perfect.

In the sunshine of 20 years ago Lee Harvey Oswald may not have killed only John Kennedy, a president. He may have slain a national soul, and a dream of a world made perfect.

1975

THOSE AWFUL GOOD OLE DAYS

'Twas a softer, slower, better time. The Good Ole Days for which everyone yearns. It was one of the times to which pessimists point when they say the world is going to the devil in a liberal-pampered society-big government-communist conspiracy-lawless-unChristian-evil handbasket.

Fifty-two years ago. A better time when there was trust among men, when you could walk the streets safely, when kids were seen not heard, when women were honored, when authority had respect, when people were happy.

Nonsense, of course. People just never remember the hard times of the Good Ole Days. The world, I submit, always has been a monstrously impossible place to live. Pick any date in recorded history and people have substantially the same troubles they have today.

I have read three ancient yellowed newspapers of July 26, 1923, a date in Fort Worth, when the temperature hit 104 degrees, the city was completing its first 18-hole golf course and Aagie Wayne Concordia, a milch cow, set a new state record by producing 814 pounds of milk in seven days.

But life was not all that simple and good. Crime was unabated. In Beaumont a teenager hacked up a doctor with an ax. Fort Worth had a $12,000 jewel robbery. An ex-constable was shot four times. A mother was accused of trying to poison her three-year-old son. She collapsed on the witness stand.

Banks were failing. Inflation, in a time when the average family income was about $1200 yearly (and families were larger), was a constant worry, not only in America but around the world. Germany particularly had troubles. It took 100,000 marks to equal a dollar and most banks could not cash a $10 bill.

Unions were agitating and striking. Steel workers wanted $3.20 for an eight-hour day. (In Fort Worth, Chamber Manager Ireland Hampton said he had had only two vacations in 25 years and the eight-hour day was "bunk.") In Boston, telephone company employees were striking and marching because of poor working conditions.

A total of 1.8 million people were jobless in England. France teetered on the edge of bankruptcy. In the Philippines, there were riots and political turmoil.

The local manager of the telephone company defended poor service to Fort Worth citizens, saying phones in foreign countries were far worse. He expected an increase in costs.

Meachams had dresses—called Tub Frocks—at $5.90 each, and better wash dresses at $9.75, which, you will notice in those inflationary times, was at least three, possibly four days worth of salary for the average family.

Teenagers were publicly admonished. The Fort Worth Cadet Band "misbehaved," said the school board, on a train trip to West Texas. There shall be no more out-of-town trips for the band, the board decreed. People complained of the drunks on downtown streets, and there were horrible accidents—in Europe 160 people died in a train wreck.

The Fort Worth Cats, in that mid-summer time, were two games ahead in the Texas League race, and you could ride the Red Ball Stage Line (actually a kind of small bus) to Mineral Wells—it was a four-hour trip ("We stop five minutes at the Weatherford Ladies Rest Room.")

America's troubles in Europe—no one respected the United States anymore, said one report—were blamed on the Republicans, chiefly President Warren G. Harding, who in this July was out of the country, in Canada and Alaska.

And a soldier, emotionally scarred by the recent war, shot and killed his doctor.

See. Nothing really changes. Like sex, for example.

Some people would have you believe morals have evaporated in the heat of the 70s, that long ago there were no problems at all with sex.

Then why was San Antonio called America's most sinful city, with a wide open red-light district, never-close saloons, and gambling houses?

In Fort Worth, personal columns were filled with messages about the town's massage parlors (Madame Pulliam, Magnetic Masseuse, Psychic Reader).

In those days, the doomsters will tell us, women knew their place. Did they? It was bobbed hair time. Dress hems were rising ("This year's hemline is about where last year's neckline was," said a columnist.) President of the United Lutheran Church said, "The American girl is at her lowest ebb in history." Immoral, he said, the women were. They drank cocktails and smoked cigarettes. "Sufferage and this New Freedom damns them," he concluded. Cisco citizens complained because teenagers were being immoral in parked cars on country lanes near that town. At Denison the KKK rode at night and intimidated young people parking and sparking.

Politically, nothing is new. Teapot Dome was stewing. In Texas, a congressman was on trial (in Comanche) for libel.

Communists were dividing Germany politically and agitating in Italy, where a few dissenters were shot. One New York family sailed for France to resettle, saying there no longer was any personal freedom in America.

The IWW—the Wobblies—scared everybody. "Reds," Fort Worth's police chief said, warning that any IWW member who set foot in his town would be arrested. So much for civil rights.

Texas' legislature was squabbling over school budgets, trying to work out a scheme for free textbooks (which some considered "communistic"). There were arguments about college textbooks, about the subversive material in them.

Prominent preacher J. Frank Norris (who later shot and killed a man) was lecturing in Cleburne on evolution. Members of one still-growing church denomination were saying for the umpteenth time that all the signs were right for the end of the world—"last evil days" was the catch-phrase.

The new silver dollar was said not to be worth the effort to mint, worthless in value. In Chicago, independent oil men blamed major oil companies for pushing up the price of gas. Farmers were complaining about poor prices for their crops, especially wheat, for which they were getting only $1.70 a bushel. Senators were calling for American isolationism and getting out of any involvement with European allies.

And the drug problem. In Brownsville, a man crazed on marijuana (said to be "obtained from dried leaves of a Mexican weed") stabbed five people. But the worst problem was with another drug—liquor. It was Prohibition and most citizens were ignoring the law and drinking anyway. In Denver, a priest was arrested for smuggling whisky into that state. Ohio's governor gave sheriffs and mayors 60 days to stop bootlegging or get out of office. Ads filled newspapers with magic medicines for restoring vigor—unstated was the fact that most were alcohol-based. In Fort Worth, a doctor was on trial for prescribing too much liquor.

If there was anything good in the papers that day in history it was the story of two runaway lovers from San Antonio. She was 17 ("over-developed physically, under-developed mentally," her mother said). He was 21 and AWOL from the Army. They were in love, intended to be married. Police caught them here.

From his cell, he said, "I love her. She is as pure as the first day her baby fingers caressed her mother's cheek. I want the world to know her purity is unsullied despite the fact we were together for two days before our arrest."

Honest. That's what he said. She said ". . . even if he has done wrong in the past I know I can make a man of him."

She concluded, "We both are misfits in our present environment."

Alienated youth. Little different than today. The more things change, as someone remarked, the more they stay the same.

1983

ANDROS: 'FANTASY ISLAND' WITH A HOT TUB

Under that glossy bulge of light on the dark horizon is, they tell me, Nassau, which is 15 miles, a sea and a sigh of relief away.

Over here, is a thumb of sand and palm trees in Small Hope Bay, on the eastern shore of Andros, the largest Bahamian island. It is night, which is an unimportant fact.

Over there, under the tumorous, glittering reflective globe, Nassau is a kind of K-Mart Hawaii, inelegantly extracting dollars from tourists with steel band sonatas and whirring slot machines and rum drinks burdened by cute names ("Castro's Revenge") and festooned with umbrella-shaped swizzle sticks.

Over here, is a breezy night music: the palm fronds clacking like castanets, pine needles tinkling like temple bells, the surf a timpani. That gurgling chorale you hear is the hot tub, bubbling and steaming under a snood of stars. Earlier there was a slightly magnificent sunset over the mangrove swamp.

Over here is better than over there.

Over here is infinitely better than over there.

Over here is far enough away from over there to make the Bahamas seem almost as the brochures claim they are: a lovely sprinkling of beach-fringed Atlantic islands becalmed by solitude, strewn with aloneness.

Over there, Nassau is a mass of neon and noise where one feels a depraved compulsion to attend guided tour excursions and crowded restaurants, clamorous night clubs, the gambling casino, to wallow in the fanciful frenzy of it all.

Nassau causes eyes to glaze over, and common sense grows frazzled and the first thing you know, you fall into the shameful practice of buying straw baskets.

Over here, an evening of hot tub sitting is considered riotous living and one is worn to abject weariness by 9:00 o'clock. Even the goat that grazed beside the tub during sunset has turned in for the night and the three wandering beige-colored hounds have curled themselves into a triad furball under a palm tree. Earlier, I heard a frog rib-bit-ing in the mangroves, but now nothing sounds except the surf and the jacuzzi's effervescent liquid Muzak.

Out there in the dark, nothing is moving except perhaps the Chickcharnies and the Yahoos and the Bosee-Amasees, who probably do not exist, and maybe a persistent drinker or two at the rickety bar in the settlement of Calabash Bay a mile down the beach.

Now, at the outrageously late hour of 9:00, Andros seems to be the classic textbook tropical island of dreams. *Fantasy Island* with a hot tub and no cloyingly cute midgets.

There are no more deserted Caribbean islands. They are myths of the brochure writer and real estate promoter. Except for spits of sand or coral atolls fit only for crabs and shipwreck victims, available tropical islands have been subdivided and developed into little sunny Levittowns.

They will tell you there are, more or less, 2,000 Bahama islands, though fewer than 70 or so will support human life. Most can be reached only if your ship goes down offshore. The Bahamas are little different from the Caribbean island groups farther south: the Dutch West Indies, the American Virgins, the Grenadines, the Turks and Caicos. All have resorts and beachfront condos and room service. You hide in the closet for privacy.

Nassau, the principal entry port of the Bahamas, could be downtown Miami Beach. The tour operators are organized to show you reconstructed forts and prancing packs of flamingoes and coral formations through glass-bottomed boats. The casinos on Nassau and Freeport have pseudo-Vegas revue shows and restaurants pretend they serve gourmet dishes. The beaches, however lovely, are franchised out to the leasors of towels and umbrellas.

To discover even the illusion of aloneness, you must strike out for the lesser Bahama Islands: Eleuthera, Abaco, Exuma, Bimini—Andros.

Leaving the airport near Andros Town, I asked the taxi driver, "Anything to see here?"

He appeared startled by the question.

"No," he said, finally.

Good.

While maneuvering his old station wagon through the minefield of potholes covering what passes for a paved road, he told me there is no Andros Town, except as a name on maps. It was planned as a new city by developers, who flashed architects' plats and plans for condos and golf courses and shopping centers. The project vanished in a wash of indifference. Any island with nothing to see and a failed condo complex can't be all bad.

Andros is, by Bahama standards, big: 111 miles long, 22 miles wide. More than three times larger than other islands in the Bahamas. Flat, with freshwater creeks and tiny lakes, marshy, cut by swamps. The western shores are called The Mud. Apparently the name is accurate. Nothing much at all over there, except mud and marsh grasses.

Over here on the eastern coast, facing Nassau across the Gulf Stream, there are local settlements, hotels and guesthouses, a yacht basin. Around Small Hope Bay, nothing is very close to anything else, though the Calabash Bay bar is within hiking distance if you feel the need for local color, a beer and scratchy jukebox music.

Largest installation on Andros is a joint British/American military complex, an underwater weapons-testing station. Which means, probably, there are nuclear subs roaming the waters offshore. No real problem. Plenty of water out there along a mile-deep trench called, lyrically, Tongue of the Sea. It's there beyond that reef, either the second or third largest in the world, depending on which brochure writer you believe. This is a skin-diving mecca.

Scuba diving is why Small Hope Bay Lodge exists, though its mere existence here beside the reef and the Tongue of the Sea is not a compelling reason to don air tank and fins. No one forces you to skin-dive. The hot tub and the hammock are worthy alternatives.

Small Hope Bay Lodge is the oldest Bahamian out-island hostelry still under the same ownership. That's Dick Birch. He built it by hand, the main lodge, the 23 rough-hewn cabins spread under the salt pine and palm trees covering this point of land in Small Hope Bay. He's sunbrown, hair going gray, still stalking the grounds with hammer and wrench to keep his little empire operating.

Earlier, there was a first Mrs. Birch. She now operates a guesthouse and a restaurant outside Nassau. Rosi is the current Mrs. Birch. She came as a guest, stayed to marry the guy with the hammer and wrench. She began and operates a cottage industry, a batik factory that turns out exquisitely designed fabrics under the brandname Androsia.

There are children around, and their spouses, and other factotums who came as guests and never left, including one who is rumored to have been a Canadian doctor. They do odd jobs. Except for the goat and the three dogs and the Bahamian workers and the diving and snorkeling instructors, that's the cast of Small Hope Bay Lodge.

The cabins are spartan, with louvered windows, a tin shower, platform beds, a commode, ceiling fans (which seemingly have only two speeds: whumph-whumph and hurricane) and no keys. Nothing is locked up at Small Hope Bay Lodge. One cabin has a waterbed and is reserved for honeymooners.

In front of the lodge is a circle of weathered chairs and tables, a worn swing. A wooden pier holds a hut filled with air tanks. Flat-bottomed dive boats are anchored there. A few sailboats and windsurfers and skiffs are tied to the pier. Another pier has a security wall of palm fronds. It's for nude sunbathing.

Guests gather for meals and leisure in the lodge. Served family style, the meals offer lamb and chicken and freshly caught fish, salads from vegetables grown on the island. The bar is an ancient dugout canoe—named Panacea. It is an honor bar. You get what you want and mark it on the tab. If you have energy, there are a ping-pong table and a mildewed pool table and 1,000 books in several languages.

Sometimes a guitar is brought out and everyone sings or Birch shows slides of scuba divers down in the Tongue of the Sea. Or the hot tub is filled to sloshing over. Small Hope Bay Lodge is, if anything, casual.

Andros may not be the deserted dream island of the mind. But it does have a couple of the advertised ingredients: sunshine and water. The sun is constant, the water colored all tones of blue, clear and warm, and filled with rare coral formations populated by fish of extraordinary beauty.

Out there, a half-mile offshore is the Tongue, 75 feet deep, then a slanting bottom, then a drop of 7,000 feet to the ocean floor, a Grand Canyon in the Atlantic. Years ago, 1962, a world record scuba-diving descent of 462 feet was established into that submarine valley.

There, too, is the birthplace of wall diving, which is meaningful to dedicated skin divers. Down on the canyon wall, they say, is a living museum of sea fossils presented in purples and oranges, reds, blues, golds and greens, guarded by trigger and parrot fish, squirrel and butterfly fish, the giant angelfish. And curious barracuda.

Experienced divers go down deep beside the wall, to the alien territory of black coral trees, sponges, eagle rays, sea turtles, even whales, porpoises and, once, a giant squid. But Birch and his instructors teach the basics to beginners and put them 20 feet deep into a coral garden along the reef. It is a wondrous world down there. Shallow divers also explore the wreck of a World War II landing barge, which Birch sunk as a kind of underwater laboratory for curious scuba novices.

For those who prefer to stay above water, the Gulf Stream offers fishing. It's said to be good, especially if you hook a bonefish in the shallows.

There's really no need to venture off the Small Hope Bay

Lodge peninsula and its surrounding waters. But you may wish a bit of aloneness. Birch keeps a stable of rusting bikes for guests who want to pedal into Calabash Bay settlement or search for Andros Town.

Or there is the beach for walking, a mile in one direction to the settlement, 15 miles of nothing in the opposite direction. This is not the usual Bahamas' postcard beach. It is, for lack of a better term, an ugly beach, a working beach, littered with the Gulf Stream's flotsam: wine bottles from South America, soggy palm fronds, Styrofoam floats, pieces of fishnet, a log of mahogany from Central America. To walk there is to assay the strayed miscellany of this hemisphere.

No one will try to rent you an umbrella and a towel.

If the laid-back essentials of Small Hope Bay Lodge become overwhelmingly boring, then, I suppose, you could strike out in search of the Chickcharnies and Yahoos. Others have.

Andros originally was settled by Seminole Indians fleeing Spanish domination and slavery about 1790. Descendants, they say, still live on the island. Over the centuries, Indian superstitions have been passed along and still are widespread today.

Andros Town, claim those who believe in such things, failed because the developers offended the Chickcharnies, who are described as elves with three fingers, three toes, fearsome red eyes, feathers and beards. They are said to rest by hanging by their tails in cottonwood trees. Anyone, so the legend goes, who insults the Chickcharnies will have his head turned backward on his shoulders.

The Chickcharnies are more fearsome than the Bosee-Amasees, who are water spirits. They remove fish from hooks, foul fishing lines and tip over boats.

The Yahoos don't bother anyone. They just hide well, though everyone knows they are out there somewhere on the island. Yahoos are described as hairy little creatures, almost ape-like, who live in holes. Respectable people, like a couple of Navy scientists, have seen them. Two or three decades ago a large search party, complete with helicopters, searched the interior of Andros for the tribe of aborigine Yahoos.

Not one was seen, but they are said to hide very well, and still are out there waiting in the dark.

Let them wait.

The hot tub and the grazing goat and the three dun-colored sleeping dogs are mystery enough. Tropical paradises are tiring to one's civilized psyche. The goat, the dogs and I all will be asleep by 9 o'clock tonight. The Yahoos can catch the second show at Nassau's casino.

1970

TRAGEDY IN WISE COUNTY

When tourists travel westward
On highway one-fourteen
They pass through old Aurora
The town that might have been

—*Etta Bearden Peques*

". . . terrible frightening-looking
creatures [with] terrible eyes."

—*Unconvinced letter writer*

For that April dawn, the sun came off the mesquite prairie like a flipped gold coin and rolled along the sooty morning clouds. The day was the seventeenth and if ancient newspapers may be trusted, it was cool for mid-spring but clear and bright. Not a single cigar could be seen in the sky.

Because it was dawn in 1897, a time when roosters had top-sergeant voices and anyone in bed after 5:00 a.m. either had no purpose in life or no rooster, Aurora citizenry aroused early with, if not enthusiasm, at least promptness.

Aurora, on that seventeenth day of April in 1897, possessed a full cemetery and empty houses. Before the tragedies—and long before the flying cigar appeared on that wonderfully clear day—the town claimed two lawyers, one undertaker, five doctors, a picture gallery, one brass band for Sunday concerts, two cotton gins, half a dozen grocery stores, a newspaper, two hotels and three thousand people.

The citizens, just country folk, had settled along Deep Creek and built themselves a town—largest in Wise County—around and over a log cabin thrown up in 1854 by Aurora's first settler, Sam Woody. Oaks and mesquites grew on the caliche hills. This side of the square, actually southeast from the settlement, was the community cemetery, on land given by Col. Beauchamp. It had a few unmarked graves but more showed rough headstones. For serenity, the cemetery had its own private hill.

Those country folk raised wheat and cotton, vegetables in the back yard, fed their chickens shelled corn and table scraps, butchered acorn-fat hogs for winter sausage, and met each night with coal-oil lamps.

All of this was before cigars flew, before life sagged in Aurora. When the calamities arrived, boll weevils heralded the event by chewing up cotton crops. With the gins almost empty, the town's economy fared badly. Later a fire swept away half the business section. Most serious among the calamities was a spotted fever epidemic or perhaps the disease was cerebrospinal meningitis as one doctor suggested. Whatever, a score of citizens died, hundreds were maimed and other hundreds were frightened enough to flee Aurora.

The dead were buried in the hilltop cemetery, and those who left never returned.

Boll weevils, fires and spotted fever, for all their destruction, were not the assassins of Aurora. They wounded; the railroad killed. By 1890, one set of tracks had been built through Rhome, or Scuffletown as it was known, to the east. Another favored Newark, toward the southwest. Those few remaining citizens saw the once-numerous population almost depleted as workers moved to the railroad towns.

Aurora was left in the apex of steel rails and nothing. Thus, Aurora on April 17 only had its roosters for dawn calls, oil lamps for night comfort, the oaks, mesquites and caliche hills.

The sun flipped up at 5:57 a.m. but civil twilight, that period of bright light before the dawn, came about 5:30 a.m. When 6:00 a.m. arrived the big, silver-colored cigar appeared above the southern horizon. The cigar showed two gasoline engines along each side. Both turned propellers. Another prop, which "bored through the air," was mounted on top for vertical lift.

By various earlier accounts the curious airborne stogie was 200 to 300 feet long and 50 feet wide. Windows, at least seven of them, were across the bottom. A strong headlight flashed out of the nose. Depending on who reported seeing the cigar, it was piloted by one of several persons, some of whom wore blue sailor suits.

On the seventeenth, however, a Martian directed the Aurora cigar.

It came in low, over Aurora's square, then zoomed north, above Judge J. S. Proctor's house, which was perched on one of those caliche hills. The cigar struck the peace justice's windmill and exploded. Debris scattered over several acres. Among other damages, Judge Proctor's flower garden was ruined.

Aurora citizens hurried to the wreck. The pilot was badly disfigured but they could see he was not of this Earth. T. J. Weems, the U.S. Signal Service officer stationed in Aurora, was an astronomy authority. His opinion was that the pilot came from the planet Mars.

Searchers found papers in the wreckage but could not read them. The writing—if it was that—was unintelligible hieroglyphics. The cigar must have weighed several tons but observers could not identify its metal and only speculated that it was a mixture of aluminum and silver.

S. E. Hayden, a local cotton buyer, surveyed the wreck and hurried off to inform the newspapers.

Since tragedy was no stranger in Aurora, the crash of a silver-skinned cigar was not particularly unsettling. Citizens cleaned up the debris and at noon of the seventeenth, they gave the Martian pilot a Christian burial in the little cemetery on the serene hill.

The year 1897, particularly the April section, was a good one for flying cigars, optionally known as airships. Aurora was fortunate—despite the damage to Judge Proctor's windmill and flower garden—to be visited by the being from outer space. Other people had to be content with brief glances or, in a few cases, chance encounters.

April, taken altogether, was a curious month, 30 days in which the sight of flying cigars and Martians were not unlikely. In Wichita Falls, for example, a doctor announced the appendectomy he performed was an unqualified success in spite of the fact that the patient was not expected to live more than 48 hours.

Fort Worth found a body—a live body—in a gutter. That was an Irishman with a rose in his lapel. He claimed to be a leprechaun. In the small town of Cooper, a girl used a hatchet to strip two joints from her right index finger, an act she said proved her purity. Unfortunately, reported the *Fort Worth Register*, the young lady was "enciente" at the time. "Enciente" is French for "Get me to the church on time." In East Texas, cow after cow was physically assaulted by wild packs of blood-thirsty buffalo gnats.

After vampire buffalo gnats and leprechauns, flying stogies seemed almost normal. These queer airships—most everyone said they were cigar-shaped except one witness who reported the ship he saw as "whale-backed"—appeared first above cities and farms in the Midwest.

An Iowa farmer claimed one of his prize cows was rustled by occupants of the cigar he saw. German settlers in Indiana said the same aerial vehicles had been seen 30 years earlier in skies over the Old Country and were piloted by the Devil and his demons. Passengers of an Ohio River steamer, the *Marietta*, watched their flying cigar for more than an hour, or so they swore.

Texas had its Paul Revere for flying panatellas: Joseph E. (Truthful) Scully, a Fort Worth man who conducted for the Texas & Pacific Railroad. Scully, whose reputation for truthfulness and honesty was unquestioned, told a reporter he sighted a supposed airship in Wood County near Hawkins. Almost immediately, citizens reported sightings in Denison, Beaumont, Whitney, Forney, Mansfield and Dallas.

In Atlanta, near Texarkana, Jim Nelson, a farmer, saw

the thing close enough to cause his hair to stand on end. Another Atlanta citizen spoke with occupants of the cigar, one of whom told him, "We will be in Greece day after tomorrow." That witness claimed three "beings" aboard sang "Nearer My God to Thee" and passed out temperance tracts.

The Rev. J. W. Smith saw the machine at 1:16 a.m. of an April morning, just as it disappeared above Childress and sped to Amarillo. C. L. McIlhaney and a dozen other citizens of Stephenville claimed the cigar landed in Erath County and had a pilot and engineer. One Stephenville man speculated, "Is the world ready for airships?"

In Merkel, a family returning from church spied an anchor hooked to a fence. A stout rope led from the anchor to the cigar, hovering just above ground. Before their eyes, the cigar opened and a small man in a blue sailor suit slid down the rope. When he saw them he cut the rope and climbed back into the cigar's belly. The stogie flew away but the anchor was displayed in Merkel for several days.

According to the *Fort Worth Register*, which "hardly cares to repeat it," Patrick Byrnes, a railroad telegrapher, came across an airship near Putnam. Byrnes, who had a reputation as "a truthful man," was pedaling his velocipede (an early bicycle) east on what would become U.S. Highway 80, toward Cisco, when he saw a light, became curious, and stopped to investigate.

What he found was the cigar, full of blue-suited men. The ship had engine trouble. The men told him, he related to the newspaper, that they were on their way to Cuba to "bomb the Spaniards." The cigar was loaded with "several tons of dynamite." The flying ship's captain revealed to Byrnes that his craft intended to drop dynamite on the Spanish navy and destroy it.

By one o'clock on the morning of April 17, the ship was repaired. It left Byrnes and his velocipede and flew off to the Ozark Mountains where, the captain said, his crew would train for the bombings.

If a ruler is placed on a map, Aurora lies almost in a straight line between the Putnam sighting and the Ozarks. By

6:00 a.m. the cigar could have been over Aurora, just in time to destroy Judge Proctor's flower garden.

But were there two cigars? Why was the crashed Aurora cigar piloted by Martians? Had they pirated the ship seen by Byrnes from the Cuba dynamiters? And there is the story related by a pair of brothers, H. A. and B. T. Hambright. From their Rhome home, about two miles east of Aurora, the brothers told the *Register* they spied a ship (claimed to be the size of a small passenger coach) with a white searchlight in front. It was cruising, they said, about 150 miles per hour and heading west.

Anyway, some airship crashed in Aurora on April 17, 1897. S. E. Hayden informed the newspapers, and the newspapers informed the world, and the world yawned at the news of a Martian-piloted spaceship crash in the little north Texas town.

But when seven or eight decades had passed and Unidentified Flying Objects were news, someone cocked an eyebrow toward Aurora. Did it really happen?

Wise County historians, long familiar with the tale, politely cleared their throats and said, no, it never happened. It was just a hoax, folks. Honest. Few people believed them. Since newspaper stories recounted the spacecraft crash, a couple of dozen investigators arrived in Aurora seeking the truth. Those included a *Saturday Evening Post* reporter and a scientist from West Texas State University.

At that time Brawley Oates was the man to see about flying cigars in Aurora. His two-pump gas station was the downtown business section of Aurora, now a village of fewer than 200 persons, mostly folks who fled city stress but still commuted daily.

Oates sat in his eight-by-eight-square-foot station house and sold soft drinks from a fridge and gasoline from the ancient pumps. He then owned the land on which Judge Proctor lived and on which the windmill and flower garden stood. Oates raised turkeys and cactus on the wreck site.

"I've told them all that they can look at the land, do anything they're big enough to do but if they find something, it belongs to me," he said, explaining his position on the mystery.

The West Texas State University scientist, Dr. Alfred E. Kraus, a director of the school's Kilgore Research Center, visited Aurora twice. He was certain the old tale was a hoax.

During his final trip, Dr. Kraus used a metal detector to search the supposed crash site. What he found were old stove lids, rings used on horse bridles, and 1932 license plates. What he did not find were bits and pieces of a silver flying cigar.

One of the arguments against the reported crash is that Judge Proctor had no windmill. Another is that the cemetery had early maps showing where everyone was buried and the maps list no Martian graves.

Oates claimed, however, that Judge Proctor had two wells, one equipped with a rope and bucket, the other fitted with a windmill! Isla Finlayson, a Rhome resident who took care of the cemetery, said the early maps did not list all burials. Many persons were buried without headstones.

"There are a lot of people out there we don't know about," she explained.

Elderly residents who lived in Aurora in 1897 claimed no memory of the event. Dr. Kraus interviewed Oscar Lawry of nearby Newark. Lawry, who was eleven years old in 1897, said he knew nothing about dead Martians and crashed cigars.

Lawry had been visited by a dozen newspaper and magazine writers, one of whom offered him a "large amount of money" to verify the crash story. Lawry would not budge from what he considered the truth.

Another resident of Aurora, who was 14 at the time of the crash, said the airship tale was "a bunch of bunk!"

Still the inquiries came. Letters from almost a dozen states reached the Wise County Historical Society. The standard reply to all writers was that the story was a hoax. Few believe that.

The tale, surely, is false. A few years ago an aging railroad telegrapher confessed that the entire flying cigar business in 1897 was a joke concocted by railroad men in Iowa. When the joke reached Texas, "Truthful" Scully was chosen to initiate the story here. Byrnes' addition apparently was un-scheduled embroidery. Other sightings by non-railroad men were, we only can suppose, products of inspired imaginations.

In Aurora, news of the airships were general, and Hayden, an educated man who had written satirical pieces for area newspapers, perhaps seized the opportunity to place his city on front pages.

Hayden, who lost his wife and two of four sons in the spotted fever epidemic, had been described by one writer as an egoist, a man "who wanted to be important." He had, the description continued, imagination and "supersedure." The only available photo of Hayden, a medium-sized ordinary-looking middle-aged man, shows him standing on a cotton bale. His forefingers are hooked behind suspender straps.

If there is a clue to the hoax in Hayden's story, it is in the signal service officer's identification.

T. J. Weems actually was Jeff Weems, Aurora's black-smith.

Could anyone have seen an airship in 1897, six and one half years before the Wright Brothers flew 59 seconds and 852 feet at Kitty Hawk, and three years prior to the first launching of Count Ferdinand von Zeppelin's powered air vehicles in Germany?

It all seems too improbable, and Martians, little men in blue sailor suits, anchors and dynamite-loaded airships headed for Cuba must have been pure imagination.

Probably it was just a coincidence that the battleship Maine mysteriously was blown up in Havana's harbor in 1898. Yeah, that was probably just a coincidence. Still. . . . . .

1970

THE YEAR THAT COST US DEAR

And what kind of year did you have?

If you're average you paid twice as much interest as principal on your mortgage, school shoes cost you about what our great-grandfather paid for a good horse and you decided that it would have been better to have loved and lost.

A rainy day year. In the supermarket corn flakes outgained AT&T. Snap, crackle and poop. Steak went back into the glass counters, like a diamond display at jewelry stores. Or for all it mattered to you, a museum exhibit of things lost.

Bologna never tasted better. And what this country needs is a cheap substitute for margarine.

If you are average your car is 5.5 years old, you experienced 7.3 days of television set trouble, you own eight dress shirts and there is a leaky faucet somewhere in your house. The leak has been there for more than four months.

The man who claimed a bird in hand was worth two in the bush never held one. An analogy for stock market brokers now serving as department store clerks.

If you are average you are at that in-between income. Too wealthy for welfare, too poor to get away from it all in the Bahamas.

The struggling average guy has courage, like one I know who sent his boss a Christmas card stamped by the company postage meter.

To save a buck the average family was reduced to cutting out frills, like clothes and hairdressing appointments for the wife, movies, candy and toys for the children. The husband did his share by not buying gas for the lawn mower, letting his wife—not a laundry—do his shirts, and not replacing the rusty garbage can.

It was a year in which the neighbors could be pitied. If you had trouble keeping up with them, think how tough it must have been for them to stay ahead.

For all the problems, though, 1970 was a healthy year. There's nothing quite as effective for getting a sick man out of bed, on his feet and back at work as having a big layoff at the plant.

The year was not good for new marriages, particularly after June when the price of rice went up.

Inflation made paper sack lunches respectable and potato chips as costly as blue chips. It made us realize that two can live as cheaply as one but only half as long.

A smart wife was one who wisely spent her food budget to serve hamburger only six nights a week. And no eating out. This past year when wives dressed for dinner, it was an apron.

The average American husband in 1970 forgot about replacing the color television set, the car, golf clubs and his wife. The average American wife gave up trips to Europe, fur coats, emerald rings, exclusive dresses, summer camp for the children, and the fun of spending money.

Mixed emotions in 1970 was robbing your kid's piggy bank to make a United Fund donation.

1970 was the year we will remember as a year when a $5 bill became small change, penny candy cost only a dime, and, during Christmas shopping, you spent more to park than on Uncle Arnold.

Inflation, of course, is just a drop in the buck, and a living wage is a little bit more than we are making.

Thirty years from now, when your grandchildren ask how tough were things during the big recession of 1970, just tell them, not tough at all. They won't believe you anyway.

1982

THE BEST MAN EVER WORN
OUT BY A NEWSPAPER

*This is the official obituary of a remarkable man. It was writ-
ten prematurely, for he continues to live long after it was prepared and warehoused in the* Star-Telegram *computer. Rich
also formally approved his obituary. When visiting our offices,
in his eighties, he was in the habit of rummaging around in
my desk drawers where he found a copy. He read it carefully,
made one minor correction, and marked it "OK."*

When a legend dies, and one has, there is a need to
search out landmarks along the path of his life, to commemorate and dramatize the man's heroic deeds.

There are almost no significant signs beside C. L. Richhart's road, except dusty envelopes of yellowed clippings in
our files, and those stories under his byline tell little of him
but that he was a particularly competent reporter for 47
years.

It is useless to look outside. No monuments, no marble
steles or granite cenotaphs are dedicated to Richhart's intrep-
idness. He neither built nor conquered, neither unearthed
treasures nor vanquished society's diseases and ills, for those
are the exploits of heroes, and Rich was not a hero, only a
legend.

What C. L. Richhart did was far more important in life
than the handiwork of heroes. What Rich did was improve
the quality of life for all those who knew him. What he did
was make people happy.

When one seeks guides to the genius of Richhart, there

are an irritatingly large number of options and a confusion about which door to enter first.

Do you begin with the smelly, putrifying whale or the eunuch on the motorcycle? Or the stolen train? The naked Sally Rand encounter?

Perhaps we should just start at the beginning. Clarence L. Richhart was born Jan. 22, 1902, in Moweaqua, Ill., an altogether conventional genesis for what would become a highly unconventional man.

As a child in Shreveport, he sold newspapers on street corners, and when his family moved to Texas, worked during his early high school teen years on the Electra *Star-News*. In Fort Worth, Rich began the city's first permanent high school newspaper, the *Paschal Pantherette*. The *Pantherette* was a private unofficial venture but when it finally began making money, Richhart, perhaps as a portent of things to come, gave the newspaper to the school. No charge.

Later, he became Texas Christian University's first sports information director, and then joined the *Star-Telegram*, first as a part-time sports writer, then as a permanent and full-time newsman. He would stay 47 years, until his retirement in 1967, being, in his words, "only a reporter." Which is like saying Rachmaninoff was just another piano player.

A newspaper office and Richhart were instantly and always compatible, for the news business is tolerant of practicing eccentrics and allows a certain nonconformity which would scandalize other, lesser businesses. From the beginning, Richhart was a non-conforming heretic of conventional lifestyle.

In manhood, Rich was gnomic with prankish eyes and the soul of a gypsy. His irregular hours gave him the complexion of a morgue attendant but there was an infectious laugh, the breezy nervous energy, a perpetual motion mind, the eternally optimistic spirit.

He was never on time, neither for work nor assignments, was ever broke and happy, always helping others, usually with *Star-Telegram* money, which he considered his to do with as he pleased.

In that, he was little different than Amon G. Carter Sr., the *Star-Telegram* founder and publisher whose early grand lifestyle was funded almost entirely by the newspaper. Richhart became a shadow image of Amon, became a kind of do-all for the publisher because, when not distracted, he was a highly competent reporter and, said a colleague, "the best public relations man on the staff." In all his life, nobody ever didn't like C. L. Richhart.

Rich's most obvious trait was his studied disregard of orthodox dress. "I always visualize Rich as an elf with the exhausted remnants of a cigar protruding from a plastic cigar-holder clamped in his teeth," once wrote Phil Record, the *Star-Telegram*'s associate executive editor who was a copyboy when he first encountered the irrepressible Richhart. "He looked as though he had gone into the closet blindfolded to select the day's wardrobe."

Like most everyone else, Amon at first tried to change Richhart. The publisher surveyed his reporter's shabby clothes and unkempt appearance and ordered Rich to upgrade his wardrobe. Rich immediately bought a suit off the rack and cavalierly ordered the haberdasher to send the bill to Amon.

Thus introduced to the marvelous ways of Richhart, Amon Carter acquiesced and learned to use Rich's considerable talents. It was Richhart to whom Amon turned when he wanted a train stolen.

After World War II the French sent thanks for America's help in the form of a Friendship Train, which toured the country laden with Gallic exhibits. Fort Worth and Amon had packed boxcars with foodstuffs for European war relief in 1943—Columnist Drew Pearson reported that Amon delayed the train while he had "Fort Worth: Where The West Begins" stamped on flour sacks. But the post-war Friendship Train was not routed through Fort Worth. The ingratitude angered Amon and he commanded Rich to go get it.

In Austin, Richhart somehow convinced French and Texas officials to bring the train to Fort Worth. Afterwards, promised Rich, the train would be returned to its regular route. The train was delivered and Fort Worthers were gratified. Then the French asked for their train back. "To hell with them," said Amon. They had to come after it.

When not doing little things for Amon, Rich had the usual reporting duties, except that no one ever knew where he was supposed to be.

A morning city editor once asked his counterpart on the afternoon edition, "Can I borrow Richhart for an assignment?"

"Borrow him? I thought he worked for you!"

Rich, with a Bedouin's loathing for permanency, belonged to no man, but flitted hither and yon, disappearing and reappearing with the whim of a playful breeze. Because he was always late for work, then-city editor Jack Butler wasn't disturbed when Rich telephoned early one morning.

"Did you find those stories I left?" asked Richhart.

"Yes."

"I'll be a little late. I ran into a fellow who wanted me to go to a chuckwagon breakfast."

"That's OK," said Butler, "but I want you to check out a story and call me."

Long pause.

"From Stamford?" "Stamford!" moaned Butler, visualizing the ranching community 150 miles west of Fort Worth.

"Well, I told you it was a chuckwagon breakfast," said Rich.

Each New Year's Eve Rich celebrated the event with a curious ritual. He ran through the newsroom ringing a cowbell, a practice that irritated night news editor Cal Sutton. One holiday season, Richhart was sent to Mexico City on assignment and Sutton anticipated the quiet evening.

Precisely at midnight, the telephone rang. A deskman answered and motioned to Sutton, "It's for you."

"Hello," said Sutton.

Over the wires from Mexico City, he heard, "Happy New Year!!!" Clang, clang, clang.

The 1936 Texas Centennial was celebrated in Fort Worth with the Frontier Fiesta featuring big show business stars, including Sally Rand, the country's best nude act. Rich was as-

MR. G.L. RICHHART

signed to write a feature story about Sally. He went to her dressing room, knocked and was summoned inside where he found Sally, naked, lying on her stomach reading the Bible. Sally stretched, rolled over and shyly covered her mons veneris with what Rich later described as Psalms 35:17. You could look it up.

In the 1940s, the *Star-Telegram* went to war. At least most of the men did, and James R. Record, the newspaper's editor, reluctantly began hiring women, of whom he did not approve as reporters. The female-dominated staff soon became known as "JRR's Harem." For the 1942 Richhart-inspired office Christmas party, the women dressed in harem costumes, complete with diaphanous pantaloons and bare stomachs. JRR blushed. While the women danced, Richhart played his trump card. A black porter dressed in the costume of a palace eunuch had been secreted in the newspaper reference room. At Rich's signal, the eunuch roared into the city room on a motorcycle, circled desks—and a disapproving, hurrumphing JRR—and disappeared down the hall.

Christmas was special for Richhart. For one thing, he was Christmas tree editor. Amon designated Rich to go to the high mountains of New Mexico and Colorado each year and choose the 100-foot-tall pine that became the community Christmas tree in Burnet Park.

One Christmas Rich selected a tree, then met a man on his way to Seattle. Richhart, having never seen Seattle, went with the guy.

There were other curious assignments, such as interviewing a promoter with a dead, decaying whale (Rich held his nose the entire time), but his main concern became the Trinity River canalization, a pet project of Amon's who imagined ocean liners docked in downtown Fort Worth. Rich wrote his first Trinity River story in 1930, the last in 1970, and for 40 years earnestly, and quite often unobjectively, pumped for development of the stream into a major inland waterway. For his work Southern Illinois University honored him with its national award for distinguished writing in maritime journalism.

When at long last Congress approved and funded the Trinity River canal project, Rich dug into his desk, removed a worn and aging package. Inside was a fancy yachting cap which he bought decades earlier for just such an occasion. He set the cap at a rakish angle on his head and strutted around the office.

Through it all, his idiosyncratic behavior was overshadowed by a gentle sweet humanity. His kindnesses to others are legion. There was an editor whose young son died of cancer. The parents returned from the funeral expecting to find a lonely, empty house, and discovered instead Rich sitting on the front steps with food and himself to help pass the long sad day.

Jack Butler was drafted into the Navy and the first wartime Easter was lonely for his wife, Mary Lou, left to manage one small child and pregnant with another. She was visited by Catherine Gunn, whose husband, Stanley, a *Star-Telegram* Pacific war correspondent, had been killed months earlier.

The women were alone, neither in a festive mood, until Richhart arrived. He came by taxi, with corsages for the women, Easter eggs for the children, and of course the best gift of all: himself.

Colleagues who learned of that Easter generosity were sure he charged the taxi ride to the *Star-Telegram*, plus, to be sure, a sizable tip. Richhart traveled everywhere by taxi on *Star-Telegram* money, or was driven by friends. Rich did not drive, itself a heresy in Texas where space and distance demand a vehicle. No doubt the *Star-Telegram* paid for it all, because Richhart traveled first class on the newspaper's money.

The classic example of Rich's easy ways with the newspaper's money was the *Star-Telegram* Employees Association picnic of 1948, not coincidentally the last outing underwritten by the paper. The association was formed in 1939 and management agreed to fund an annual picnic. The $1,000 or so, believed Amon, was money well-spent, and the picnic always was a pleasant outing with potato salad and lemonade and softball games.

In 1948 Rich was elected association president, thus in charge of the annual picnic. The site he selected on Lake Worth had a beach and sports facilites and old pavilions. He believed the buildings were a little shoddy and hired carpenters to spruce them up. A bog of quicksand was found and workers engaged to bridge the dangerous patch. He contracted with a caterer and declared the picnic would go on for thirty-six hours because the newspaper had two staffs. Buses were leased to move reporters from the office to the picnic. There were speedboat rides and seaplane flights, goat carts for the kids, hayride wagons, hourly drawings for prizes, floor shows by the Flying X Ranchboys, free liquor and gambling at a pavilion Rich outfitted as a casino. Bands continuously played for dancing.

Rich's surprise came at sunset of the second day, as he gathered everyone on the lakeshore while across the water twilight exploded with a panorama of fireworks. Rockets soared and burst in sparkling showers, bombs shattered the night, blossoming fiery sky missiles spread fingers of reds and greens and blues—a classic fireworks display. But more was coming.

There above the water etched in fire dozens of feet high and, as a reporter later wrote, 'Lighting up the night sky for miles around,' was the flaming portrait of Amon G. Carter Sr.

Onlookers were stunned and within the silence was an astonished voice, "Damn! What next?"

Next was the bill, $12,000. When the costs were assembled and totaled, a seething Amon summoned Richhart.

"I guess what we oughta do," shouted Amon, "is make you a gawddamned vice president in charge of finances!"

Rich later denied it but he, either ignoring or dismissing Amon's sarcasm, allegedly answered, "I dunno. What's it pay?"

That Richhart could mount an extravaganza was not surprising to anyone who had visited him at home where his house was a kind of salvage Disneyland.

When he and his wife, Lucille, moved there in 1935 it was a five room, one-story cottage. Richhart had a kind of genius for junk and castoffs, and began expanding. First was an apartment house for his mother, then an extension on one side of the structure. When his youngest son took a bride, a quaint honeymoon cottage sprang up in the back yard, converted from what once had been a Silk Stocking Row carriage house. At some point the back yard took on the look of a New Orleans courtyard with vines entangling limestone columns Rich scrounged from a Summit Avenue mansion. He bought 100 huge doors from the old St. Joseph's Hospital, housed them out back. There were stained glass doors and chandeliers from the Broadway Presbyterian Church, iron gates and floor-mounted stools from a downtown cafe. A 30-foot hackberry grew larger and larger and over the house and when Rich built a second story he simply enclosed the tree. That became a problem each fall when leaves fell inside the house and he raked the floor. The roof leaked—as many as 15 buckets often were needed to catch the drips—and Rich's practical solution was to build a carportlike canopy over the whole house.

Out back lived wild animals—"Every possum in Fort Worth stays here," he once said—and Rich tolerated them. He even treated the ants gently, often leaving them breadcrumbs. Rich enjoyed his gardenlike patio.

Rich entered old age as he had lived, indomitable, bearded, balding, as blithe as an imp, forever irrepressible, a wondrous little man.

In 1974 he and his wife of 50 years, Lucille, celebrated their golden wedding anniversary. Half a century earlier they had married in the old Central Methodist Church, which had become the Panther Boys Club; on the spot where the altar once stood was a boxing ring.

Rich and Lucille donned boxing gloves and met in the center of the ring. She cold-cocked him.

Lucille died in August, 1980, and Rich came to the *Star-Telegram*—in a taxi—to personally oversee the obituary. He was bent with age and his hearing was bad and he spoke of things long ago, his wife, the newspaper, his friends.

A newsman drove him home and before leaving the car,

Rich said, "I'll die soon." There was no sadness, no regret in his voice. Just a statement of fact: "I'll die soon."

And so he did, and today his friends will remember. Some will cry but most will recall a favorite Richhart story and smile.

In death, Rich was as giving as he was in life. His body was willed to a medical research center.

There are no monuments for this legend, merely friends, because to paraphrase Mark Twain's assessment of a fellow reporter on the *Virginia City Enterprise*, C. L. Richhart was the best man ever worn out by a newspaper.

Another now-dead *Star-Telegram* reporter, Alf Evans, spoke a telling epitaph about Amon Carter Sr., which is fitting for Rich:

"I don't know where he is today but wherever he is, the people there are having a good time."

1978

COWBOYS

I and they were but creatures of circumstances—the circum-
stances of an unfenced world.

—Anonymous Cowboy

Credo quia absurdum—
  I believe it because it is absurd

—Traditional

You may forget the singer,
but don't forget the song.

—Traditional

Lan Twohig cost his daddy six bits and a lifetime supply of syphilis. His daddy paid the one and collected the
other to and from Miss Molly Hipp on a bed of corn shucks
spread in an open oxen cart somewhere on the road between
Indianola and San Antonio. The year was 1842, when the
Texas Republic was young and healthy, and Ms. Hipp was
neither. Lan Twohig's daddy surely received the disease because when Molly Hipp died a year later her death was attributed to chronic syphilis and alcoholism, and possibly the
.44 caliber hole above and slightly to the left of her nose.

In later years Lan, always more jolly than he had a right
to be, joshed that he and his daddy had two things in common. Neither ever saw the other and each had stayed with
Molly Hipp less than twenty minutes. Ms. Hipp carried Lan
the usual term, then dropped him in the rear room of a brothel
beside San Pedro Creek in San Antonio. The midwife, a rented
Mexican lady, took Lan home after Molly looked on her new
son and said tenderly, "Get rid of it."

Lan lived out his first year among the midwife's natural children. She passed him to pious nuns of San Juan Mission who doled him out to an Indian family within the mission compound. In his sixth year the nuns, feeling they could tolerate his wicked illegitimacy no longer, dealt him to a farming couple, Mattie Mae and John Golson, who worked 160 acres near Seguin, east of San Antonio. The Golsons were mediocre farmers, poor parents and only middling with acts of quasi-kindness toward Lan. They gave him his first real clothing, cured his cornmush-created malnutrition, presented him with a name—Enoch—and a basic education in the community log school.

John didn't last long enough for Lan to get used to him. The farmer died in the cold February of 1849. Mattie Mae became marm of the school. She was well beyond her prime, a slit-mouthed, icy-eyed woman, who tut-tutted loudly at life's crimes against her, of which there were many but especially Lan. The nuns thoughtfully had told the Golsons of Lan's corn-shuck pedigree and Mattie Mae soon came to feel the small thin boy was a special cross sent to test her faith. She alternately beat and prayed the devil out of Lan. He endured the beatings and cascades of tuts because life, he believed, was like that. From his eighth year Mattie Mae taught him the value of hard work by renting him by the day to neighboring farmers.

In 1855, Lan Twohig *né* Enoch Golson, thirteen, small and thin but infused with an inner toughness, again was alone. Mattie Mae tutted her last. Pneumonia. Lan did not wait for fate to pitchfork him again but gathered his few possessions, Mrs. Golson's life savings of $53, and found the nearest road, which incidentally took him south.

Where Lan roamed for the next 40 years or so I do not know with any certainty. He became a cowboy, a *Texas* cowboy, which was the original model. The then-new profession was being created by men who practiced severe anonymity, and whose lives were less romantic and adventuresome than John Wayne has led us to believe. The cowboy, or "cow boy," as the term was written before he began riding on Hollywood's purple celluloid landscapes, was a kind of Cossack in service of the prairie czars then inventing the American cattle industry. His forefathers were the Spanish Conquistadores, his cousins, the mountainmen who first ventured into the West. And he was, says historian Paul Horgan, ". . . the last of the clearly traditional characters [born] from the kind of land he worked in and the kind of work he did."

He neither built nor explored nor populated the West but moved ever so briefly across it, as capricious and lonely as the blowing dust. Dime novelists and penny dreadful authors scribbled magniloquent lies about the cowboy for rapt eastern readers but saw him only in town, often ending long cattle drives with a few desperate hours of extravagant carousal before returning to a life of social desolation. Like a cloistered monk of some distant forgotten monastery, the cowboy served his god, the rancher, and toiled at labors decidedly unglamorous. Moving often from ranch to ranch, the cowboy made few lasting friendships. He was untutored and ignorant. For endless months he lived on the range, burned in summer, frozen in winter, as punished as the cattle he attended. He slept on the ground under "hen-skin" blankets. He arose at 4:00 a.m., or earlier, and often was not asleep again until midnight. He was fed a constant diet of beans—"Pecos strawberries," greasy stews and Arbuckle's coffee. His aches and sprains were treated with heavy coats of axle grease or prickly pear poultices. To stay awake during long nights of riding herd, he rubbed tobacco juice in his eyes. He lived in a society of men and made love to the only available women, the ubiquitous "soiled doves" and "Fallen Angels," on almost a seasonal basis, like some animal in heat. He smelled of the horse he rode, of the cows he tended, and the dung of both. Miasmic as a nocturne, the cowboy was a neutered man, often profane, never profound, illiterate, itinerant—a harsh child who went crooked, stayed straight, or alternated, like an electric current. He hid his past behind such curious aliases as "Shanks" and "Pieface," "Muley," "Stormy," and "Joggy." He observed no religion but the trinity of cow, horse and land. For his always-brief entry into towns, he exploded

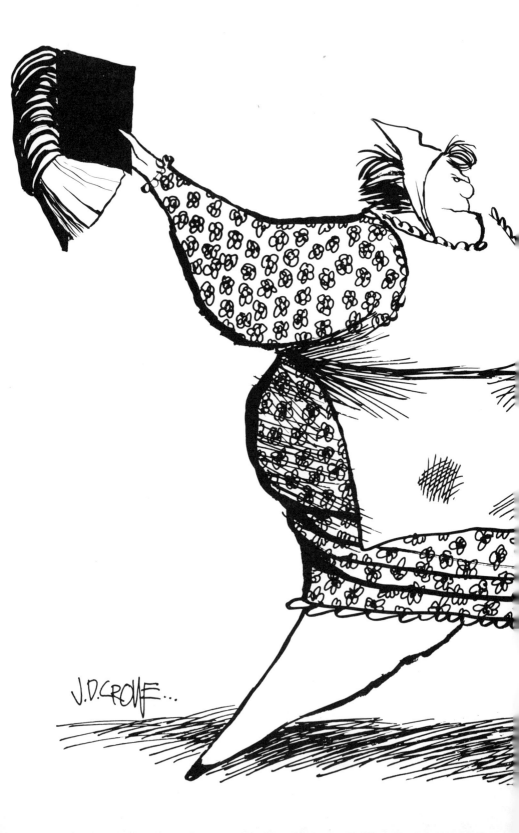

J.D.CROWE...

MATTIE MAE GOLSON
RELIGIOUSLY BEATING
THE DEVIL OUT OF LAN.

with drunkenness and venery, exchanging six months' wages
for a few hours of release from his Trappist confinement. His
was a "soulless, aimless" existence, wrote one of the few in-
trospective cowboys who left the range world when he saw it
for what it was.

No American character endured as the cowboy, though
the cowboy of Hollywood and Zane Grey was nothing like
the reality. The cowboy lasted little longer than The West, as
few as twelve, perhaps as many as a score of years. Behind
him came the men with hoes and plows and wives. The cowboy scorned the new arrivals, but the farmer lasted; the cowboy did not. He went away to other jobs, went away to other
truths and, finally, he just went away.

So it must have been for Lan Twohig.

As many cowboys, Lan buried his past by assuming another name. His final and lasting name came, he said, from an
old man, Albert Twohig, and Landers, a foreman for Shanghai Pierce. Lan said he rode with Pierce in South Texas and,
immediately after the Civil War, helped the rancher move a
cow herd to New Orleans. Pierce and his friend, Captain
Richard King, whose ranch would become the world's largest,
were a pair of those feral Caesars then composing the cattle
industry. Pierce was a huge man whose voice, cowboys said,
could be heard a mile distant. He became a legend with antics
as, during a late-in-life trip abroad, trying to visit His Holi-
ness, the Pope, unannounced. Swiss guards forced him out of
the Vatican with drawn bayonets.

Lan sold cattle to King and Pierce, Longhorns he had
gathered, perhaps illegally, on open ranges, and Longhorns he
chased and trapped in the barbarous land called the *brasada*.

Nothing ever said of the Texas Longhorn was an exag-
geration. It came from where every mean and marvelous
thing of Texas came, from the malignant, iniquitous brush
country—the *brasada*—above the Rio Grande. It was a tortuous Eden, a natural savage wilderness without relief from
the Nueces River to the Mexican border. Every living thing
inside fought for its place. There were mesquite, both bush
and tree, with dirk-like thorns, and the Spanish dagger, walls

of prickly pear cactus which to O. Henry seemed as ". . . large, fat hands," yellow blooming *huisache*, and the catclaw called by Mexicans "Wait-A-Minute" because it grabbed and held. Either dusted with fine gray blowing sand or, wrote Horgan, "beaten by deluges that hissed as they first struck the hot ground," the brush country was a haven for nature's angry misanthropes—the quill-backed peccary, the rattlesnake, the Longhorn. Virtually waterless and endless to a man on horseback, the *brasada* was a maze of interlocking thickets enclosing small clearings. There were wandering paths worn to dust by animals but many dead-ended and few men knew a safe route. It was for this barbarism of a land that the first cowboys, who were Mexicans, devised leather leggings called chaps. Without protection, the brush would claw a man to pieces.

In its brush country sanctuary, the Longhorn was an evil thing. Evolved from strayed Moorish cattle, the Longhorn, J. Frank Dobie wrote, was the ". . . parody of a cow." It had elk legs, could outrun a horse, was bony, high at the shoulders, low at the tail, shaggy-haired, gaunt-rumped, with a goat-limber neck holding a massive head from which grew horns curved like twin scimitars. In a wild state, cowboys claimed, the Longhorn lived on wind and gravel. An adult bull weighed twelve hundred pounds and more of muscle and bone, and a few stood as tall as a man on horseback. Angered or wounded, it feared nothing and once provoked, would attack anything, even the black bears that roamed Texas. Should its victim escape, the Longhorn followed indefatigably with its nose to the ground sniffing the trail like a wolf. The wild Longhorn had no herd instinct, but kept a few wives for which he was a fierce champion. At sunset he called his family together for the night and his bellow, heard by cowboys camped in the *brasada*, was fearsome, chilling—the roar of a true wild beast.

The Longhorn was never civilized. It was chased down, dragged to corrals, herded, branded, conditioned to a gentler environment, but never tamed. Man and Longhorn at best held an uneasy peace. Gathered on the unfenced ranches of

Southwest Texas, the Longhorns foraged on sweet grasses, multiplied, spread over Texas, and became an industry. Soon after the Civil War, when Northerners cried for meat, ranchers began driving their Longhorns to Kansas railroads. "Them Longhorns," said an Oklahoma rancher of this century, "could live on nothing, and you could drive them to market and it didn't hurt 'em because they wasn't any good to begin with." The Longhorn's meat was sinewy and gamy but it was beef and northern stomachs complained little.

The era of cattle drives lasted fewer than a dozen years. Railroads came to Texas. Barbed wire enclosed land. Foreign cattle, the Herefords and Angus with fat bodies and stubby legs, were introduced. By the late 1880s, most Longhorns had been bred away, though a rancher might keep a dozen for old times sake. In distant reaches of Texas, a few wild Longhorns survived but slowly they died or were killed by cowboys to protect the pureblooded cows and, then, as the cowboys, they were no more.

Late in life, Lan Twohig was a windy man, given to bragging, so his claim of invincibility in the *brasada* perhaps was untrue. He said he was the best man ever to chase Longhorns in the brush, better even than the Mexicans who felt a mystical kinship with the wild cattle. Lan bragged he feared nothing the bush land offered. He entered with a short rope and a pistol, often afoot if the bull had come to a fighting place. He was a sure roper with the braided lariat and quick enough to escape the Longhorn's charge.

Other cowboys went in pairs, even by fours, to chase down, surround and capture the worst of the bulls. Lan went alone. He had a sense of survival, an innate grasp on the Longhorns' souls. He could track them even in the rocky stretches that left no hoofprints, intuitively following the correct trail. He knew their habits, their instincts for escape. He knew the moment they would turn and fight, and he was ready with the rope or, when necessary, the pistol. Once seen, a Longhorn had no secrets from Lan. He knew how it would charge, how low or high the horns would be carried, how the animal hooked, how it turned, how desperately it would struggle against the cowboy.

Lan remembered the *brasada* and its fierce Longhorns as the best time of his life.

He sold the live cattle to ranchers, the dead ones for their hides, and occasionally worked on ranches. Mostly, Lan was just a cowboy. In 1867, he rode with one of the first cattle drives to Kansas and later accompanied four other herds before growing weary of the trail. He wandered from ranch to ranch, cowboying for the Double Moon, the G-4 near Marfa, the Rocking C in the Panhandle. Lan saw little cash money, was alone and often lonely, never married. In the late 1880s, he went beyond the Pecos to become the sole gringo cowboy on Moody's place. I do not know Moody's other name but he operated a ranch above the Rio Grande, probably on the eastern fringe of the Big Bend.

Lan, in those years, was an economized man in stature, manner and speech. His eyes were blue over a flattish nose. There was graying thin hair, the weather-pinched face and morning aches, but Lan was muscular, quick with his movements, hard and strong for his size.

In 1892, at fifty, Lan was too old for ranch life but he had nowhere else to go. In that year, he fought the bull. In that year, at dawn of a sunless autumn day, he stood before the green wall of a sandy gully, remembering the earlier better times, the *brasada*, the excitement of the brush and wild Longhorns.

Two days before, Lan had seen the bull Longhorn, a big blue dun with red flanks and huge flared horns. It lured three cows and a heifer from a pasture near ranch headquarters, took them running into the bushy hills. Lan saw the bull clearly.

"Naw," said Moody, "not one of them old bulls, Lan. Ain't none of them no more."

Wild Longhorns were few but they lasted well into the twentieth century. As late as the 1920s one lived in a narrow canyon south of Lubbock on the high plains. A Big Bend rancher killed another in 1910. A Model T Ford encountered a wild bull in the eastern mountains of New Mexico. The Longhorn stood on a rough narrow road and the driver braked hard. The bull bellowed, pawed the ground, and charged the automobile. It bashed at the car, stepped back, and charged again and again. Eventually a horn pierced the radiator and the bull actually raised the machine's front wheels off the road, shook it and bounced it into a ditch.

Lan Twohig's outlaw bull Longhorn was real.

He went after it, ignoring Moody's advice to take other cowboys with him. He found prints in a sandy wash south of the ranchhouse and tracked his bull south and eastward, deeper into the brush, finally crossing Muke Water Creek. From the shadows of a cottonwood grove he saw the heifer beside a mesquite thicket.

Throughout the night, Lan watched the brushy fortress, saw the bull move the cows into a steep-sided gully. He rode

around it. The gully dead-ended against the hill. The wash
was filled with brush, thick with mesquite and cactus. Lan
knew the bull had its nest within that thorny citadel.

And at dawn, with a thin banner of light undercoating
dense clouds, Lan stood before the green wall, lightly holding
his horse, Buck, listening to the silence. An aimless wind rif-
fled the slender mesquite leaves. Lan tied on his chaps. He
dropped a coiled rope over the saddle horn. He mounted. The
hardness of his rifle, stuffed into a leather scabbard, pushed
against his right leg.

All right, ole bull, let's me and you do it.

Lan gently touched the horse's flanks. They entered the
green barrier.

The path was a dark corridor, cool and dusty. Lan followed the trail straight for a dozen steps, turned sharply
right, circled a mesquite trunk. Then again it was a thin line
deeper into the gully. Fifty feet. He was forced to dismount as
the tree ceiling lowered. He scraped cactus and the thorny
catclaw clutched at him. A gray lizard hung to a mesquite
limb, frightened and unmoving. On the right, the brush was
thinner and Lan could see the gully's brown wall. He found
fresh cow dung and once he rubbed his hand across the
smoothed bark of a tree to which clung red hairs. He smiled.

The trail wandered as though aimless but, Lan knew, was
carefully devised. He rode when he could, walked when he
could not. The coiled rope was held lightly in his right hand.
He watched everywhere, his eyes never still. Above, Lan could
see the beige sky.

The brush thinned. Ahead was a clearing, small, oval-
shaped, twenty feet wide. He stood at its edge, shadowed by a
tree. The trail led around the clearing's perimeter. Lan listened, tensed. Across the open space, he heard movement in
the brush, then silence again. He sat easy on Buck for a long
time, waiting. Finally, Lan impatiently urged the horse into
the opening, rode slowly across and disappeared again into the
green thicket. The path was broader, and he rode a hundred
feet before having to dismount again beside a mound of
cactus.

The cry came with suddenness, loud and fierce, frighteningly intense. Lan whirled. *Behind! The bull came out and waited for me to be trapped inside!* Ahead, he heard the cows calling to the bull. Buck skittered, his teeth grinding the bit, and Lan swung into the saddle, already pulling on the rifle, dropping the looped rope over the horn. He could hear the bull outlaw thrashing in the brush, still bellowing, charging, exploding into the clearing. Buck was at full gallop as man and horse sped into the sandy open space. The bull was in the middle, mouth agape and frothy, dripping long banners of slobber, the head bent low, horns carried right atilt, cocked like an archer's bow. Its feet beat the dust into clouds.

The suddenness of the bull startled Buck, and the horse jumped to the right as horns came up in a blur, thrown like sabers. A horn struck Lan's left leg above the knee, pierced the chaps' thick leather. It entered his flesh and ripped away. The horn scraped along the thick saddle and sliced a slender line on Buck's flank. Blood instantly flowed from the long wound.

Buck's momentum carried them across the clearing as Lan reined hard. The horse stumbled in the turn, its hooves punching up showers of sand. The bull was about, charging once more. Lan twisted his body and fired, then pumped the rifle again. The bullet entered along the bull's back, high on the rump. The horse was rising from its knees. Lan fired again as the Longhorn struck horse and rider.

Later Lan would remember the sound of the impact, Buck's terrified scream of agony, horns breaking through the horse's body, and he would recall the stench of the animal and the pain. He could not forget the pain.

The bull crunched against the horse. One horn ripped into the stomach, the other broke through bones in the chest and rib cage, pushed upward to lodge against the spine. The Longhorn lifted horse and rider into the air and for a long moment held them motionless before the weight became too much. They crashed to the ground, and the bloody, dusty arena was quiet. Lan was unconscious.

Much later the pain awoke him, and he screamed. He

was on his right side, still in the saddle. Buck's body lay on his right leg. His left leg was pinned between the bull's head, gleaming red with blood, and the horse's heaving stomach. The horns were inside Buck. Lan's ankle was broken.

Enraged, the bull bellowed, stamped its rear feet, and butted hard against the enemy. Forced to its knees by the horse's weight and bound tightly by its horns locked into Buck's body, the bull could not disengage itself, could not rise. With each thrust of the head against Lan's leg, the cowboy cried aloud. Finally, he passed again into unconsciousness. During the long day, Lan was unconscious a dozen times. The bull would not cease trying to escape its impalement and each time it thrashed at the horse, Lan was driven into pain and insensibility.

He would remember pieces of the day. Once he dimly saw the cows and heifer grazing quietly across the clearing. Sometime, he did not know when, he was aware that Buck was dead. In another moment of consciousness he remembered the rifle. He swiveled his head until he saw it behind him, two feet beyond his reach. He could not see the rope.

He awakened in dim twilight to find the bull unmoving. It breathed hoarsely, almost gasping air, but no longer seeking escape. He could smell the blood, feel it beneath him, feel it caked on his clothing. He saw the rivulet of congealed blood leading to a blackened hole in the bull's rump. Lan's mouth was dry, his tongue swollen. His eyes were gritty with sand. He slept.

Lan awoke in the cool darkness, remembering the knife in his right pocket, beneath the awful weight of Buck. He tried to reach the knife. The bull tensed its legs, snorted once but did not move. Lan could not force his hand beneath the weight and he clawed at the ground with his fingers. He pulled away sand and earth, burrowing farther and farther underneath until he could feel the edge of the chaps, then more, and he touched the pocket. His fingers inched inside, grasped the material and pulled, slowly drawing out the pocket, dragging along the knife in its bottom. Then he had the knife between two fingers. He grabbed and held it tightly.

A pocketknife with two blades, but sharp enough. He opened the longer blade, grasp the hilt. He swung with his left hand, striking at the bull's head. The blade broke against the Longhorn's skull and, angered, the bull lunged forward. Lan screamed and the pain sent him away again.

The moon, full and bright, was out, centered above the clearing. Lan awoke. The pain in his upper leg where the horn had torn through was less but his ankle throbbed. The bull was still and quiet. He cursed the animal, himself, the knife-blade's weakness. He felt again for the knife and found it near his head. He opened the remaining smaller blade. Lan had another way, one he did not like. He would release the bull. He plunged the knife into Buck's flank, and began cutting.

The bull bunched its muscles in fear but did not move.

Lan took a long time to cut away Buck's side. His hand was slippery with blood. He cut back, deeper and lower, between the horse's legs, and ran his hand into the dark cavity. He could feel the horn. The bull was pulling then, helping the man free him. Lan placed the knife blade beside the horntip to cut deeper into Buck. The Longhorn pulled. Lan heard the ripping sound, felt the horn move. The bull turned its body left, backed and the right horn tore out, free again. The blunt hard head lifted from Lan's leg. The bull shook itself, rose on its forelegs and edged away, sliding out the left horn.

It stumbled once, moving awkwardly in a circle. The bull lifted its head, swung the massive, bloody horns, limbering exhausted neck muscles. It stopped across the clearing and lowered its head again, staring at Lan. Lan began digging beneath Buck's body with the knife.

Lan dug twenty minutes to loosen and pull away enough dirt for a trench. Now with most of the horse's weight on the edges of the furrow, Lan cut the tiestrings and belt of his chaps, pushing hard on the saddle. His right foot slid out of its boot. He reached behind, grasped a mesquite bush and pulled, slowly dragging himself from under the horse. He was free and lay for a moment, breathing deeply. He raised his head and looked across the clearing at the bull. The Longhorn watched Lan, studying the man with intensity.

Lan held his useless left leg and grimaced as he pivoted on his hip. He felt for the rifle, wrapped his fingers around the barrel and pulled it to him. He worked the lever and the small noise alerted the bull. It raised its head and moved right, its eyes never leaving Lan. Lan turned again on his stomach, facing the bull. He laid the rifle barrel across Buck's neck.

He could see the bull clearly in the bright moonlight, the dull, dark patches of blood, the black eyes, the horns rising from the slab head. The bull stood stiff-legged, breathing hoarsely. A muscle rippled skin along its back. It lifted a front hoof, set it hard into the dirt. Lan aimed, sighting down the barrel at the dark flat head. He tightened his finger against the trigger.

He did not shoot but held still, one eye closed, the other unblinking, staring over the gunsight. The bull waited. Lan pulled the rifle butt tighter into his shoulder, increasing the pressure. He held his eyes shut and caught his breath. His leg ached with pain. He looked again at the bull standing a dozen steps away in the thin moonlight.

He raised the rifle barrel high and fired.

And then he slept, and perhaps dreamed, for he remembered a bull crying deeply and fiercely somewhere in the brush.

Lan awoke beside Muke Water Creek, out of the bright sun. Moody knelt beside him.

"Got to wonderin' 'bout you," Moody said softly. "Came to look. I sent a hand back for the wagon."

Lan's lips were swollen, his tongue heavy and thick. His wounds had been cleaned with creek water. He hurt all over.

"It was a bull, Moody," Lan whispered hoarsely. "Like I said, old wild bull."

"You didn't get him?"

"I shot high, scared him off. Told him we'd do it agin 'nother day."

Lan smiled, and slept again.

For the remainder of his life Lan walked with a cane and never again was he an active cowboy. He stayed with Moody, working around the ranch, bossing the Mexicans. Five months after Moody found Lan in the gully, the rancher rode in with a pair of horns.

"Got somethin' for you," Moody said. "Your old outlaw's horns. Found him dead a mile above the creek."

"Sure it's him?"

"How many bull outlaws we got? It's him. Dead a month, maybe. Bones pretty well picked over but the hide's still plain. Dun with red flanks. It's your old bull."

Lan mounted the horns on polished mesquite wood and hung them above the fireplace. He often spent long evenings thinking of the bull.

Moody died in 1903. Briefly, Lan moved to San Antonio, then moved north to Fort Worth where he worked in the slaughter houses and traded cattle on the side for extra money. When he had time Lan loafed with other cowmen in the Metropolitan Hotel's regal lobby. The hotel was showing its age and one day would become a part-time whorehouse, but in 1905 it was the gathering place for cattlemen come to town. There Lan and his cronies drank too much, told lies of their youth. Lan often spoke of the bull and the gully. Other cowmen professed to believe every word of Lan's tale but many did not, even when he showed the horns for proof, pointing out the thin cuts made by his broken knife.

*   *   *   *

Was Lan Twohig real? I don't know. Amon Carter claimed the old cowboy existed, told and retold his story for audiences in the Northeast. This version came from the memory of James Farley, who was Postmaster General in the FDR administration and Amon's close friend. Amon said he bought the steer horns from Lan Twohig. I know the horns were real, for Amon showed them off to many visitors, always pointing out the marks made by Twohig's knife. For whatever reason, Amon gave the horns to Mayor Jimmy Walker in the summer of 1928 and he took them back to New York with him. Perhaps the horns still are somewhere in the city, in an attic or a basement, just relics of a long ago time in Texas, of Amon Carter and a cowboy who may or may not have lived.

1974
THE SCREWDRIVER AND OTHER DANGEROUS WEAPONS

A man who has 10 thumbs once observed that home-owners are easy to spot at cocktail parties. They are the people with Band-Aids.

A homeowner, he went on, is always just returning from the hardware store. A homeowner is a guy who never has the right tool to fix whatever it is that's broken this week. A homeowner is a man who, after trying and failing, will pay a plumber $15 to replace a 10-cent rubber washer in a faucet.

That guy also has a wife who whispers, "Now watch how he does it so we don't have to pay $15 next time."

She is the kind of wife who complains to cocktail party partners that she comes from a broken home: Her husband can't fix anything. Funny.

I am considering a new organization, to be called Do-It-Yourself Anonymous. Membership is open to any home-owner whose wife has complained, "Why don't you buy things that don't break?"

In DIYA new members will learn how cruel fate has been to them. It's a proven fact. Statistics show that if you don't have the mechanical ability to change batteries in your flashlight, you will live next door to a guy who has $10,000 worth of woodworking equipment and a full set of metric tools in his garage.

Latest survey figures prove that if you don't know how to oil hinges in your front door, you'll only make friends with guys who build their color televisions from kits they sent away for.

There seems to be no place those of us without fixing abilities can turn for sympathy. We are stuck with our rusty pliers. Plumbers and electricians spend more time at our houses than in-laws.

Do-It-Yourself Anonymous would be an answer.

One of the pieces of national legislation to be proposed by DIYA would be the Screwdriver Act. Under the law's provisions all screwdrivers would be registered with the government as dangerous weapons.

When the communists take over they get the list and come to your house to confiscate the screwdriver. And the sooner the better.

Another national law to be proposed by DIYA is the Duplicate Doohickey Statute.

When that law is passed all manufacturers will have to make two of everything.

You know the routine. Something breaks. Like a special little bolt on a cabinet door. It's odd-sized, of course, so none of your wrenches fit it. You snap it off with two or three whacks of a hammer.

You go to the store that sold you the cabinet and tell the man, "This little doohickey broke. I need another one."

He looks at it. "No . . . don't believe so. They don't make those anymore."

But he'll be happy to sell you another complete cabinet door for only $97.50. That new door has a new doohickey of which there is only one in the world. Costs a nickel to make, and $100 to replace.

A neighbor who has proposed himself for DIYA membership recounts his woes with a light fixture in his all-electric home. Two light fixtures, in fact.

The first was in the ceiling of his living room. The recessed light was held in place by two small springs, one of which broke the other day. It was a tiny spring with a funny hook on one end. He went to the company that installed the lights. Nope, don't carry those things. Not extra. Got a new fixture, though. Just $22.

A week and nine lighting and hardware stores later he gave up. His fixture hangs there, shakily agape.

Outside he has one of those post lights that switch on at sunset. The electric company sold it to him. His kid broke the globe, which is maybe five bucks worth of round glass.

He went to the electric company. Sorry, it said, don't carry that. Got a new fixture for you, however. Just $50. Two weeks and dozens of lighting and hardware stores later, he surrendered.

He said he intends to saw off the light post at the ground and cover it with dirt, and maybe a little sign that says, "Rest in Peace."

When Do-It-Yourself Anonymous gets going I expect we'll be flooded with applications from weary homeowners. We can't help ourselves, maybe we can help each other.

The way it works is whenever you get the urge to fix something around the house a fellow DIYA member rushes over and hits your thumb with a hammer.

THE REV. J. FRANK NORRIS

1978

SMITING A SINFUL WORLD

Baptists, of course, were first in line to redeem Fort Worth souls. Blazing a trail into the wilderness, Baptists were there to preach the fledgling town's first sermon. Baptists built the first permanent church and later, in 1889, constructed a mammoth stone-turreted Gothic fortress for God, who was not unpleased.

By 1909 the First Baptist Church of Fort Worth garrisoned a congregation of 334 born-again souls, all correctly water-dipped and scrubbed of sin. They were an exotic bunch of reformed sinners, socially and financially elite, conservative, unproselytic, liturgically housebroken, a tamer breed of Baptists, almost like regular Christians.

In that year their preacher passed on and God sent J. Frank Norris to tend Fort Worth's tranquil Baptist flock. Tall, gangling and gawky, slender to the brink of emaciation, Norris seemed an innocuous Ichabod Crane figure until one was transfixed by his messianic eyes. Eyes of absolutism, pale blue and painful, mesmerizing. Old Testament eyes that trespassed on other men's souls.

However arresting his appearance, Norris nevertheless was a shattered man, deeply in debt, possibly consumptive, owning faith in neither himself nor God, in his words, "pale, wan, worn, and weary." Norris' fundamentalist credentials, though, were proper. He sprang from poor Warner, a central Texas sharecropper and popular drunkard, and Mary, the severe-faced mother who loved nothing better than condemning her husband's miserable soul to hell and talking to the Lord.

Mary had visions in which God appeared before her and

chatted amicably, mostly of how young Frank was to become the greatest preacher in the world. At thirteen, Frank, lean and sickly, a slender spear being honed for the Lord, was creek-dipped with Baptist salvation. At eighteen, he entered Baylor University in Waco—"Athens of the Baptist World"— to graduate seven years later valedictorian of his class. Briefly, Norris pastored a Dallas church then became editor of the Baptist *Standard*, which was to Texas Baptists as Sears catalog to a West Texas farm family, a passport to all good things.

Though moderately successful, Norris burned inside for the glorious fame promised him by God and Mary. He became despondent, neurotically depressed by the Lord's failure to act on his behalf. It was then God called him to Fort Worth and he mounted the durable First Baptist Church pulpit where he uttered untroubling sermons for the comfortable congregation. So far, so good.

For two years, Norris was a nonentity, unobtrusive, unnoticed, undisturbing to his elitist brood, a preacher accepted but unexceptional. One day an ad appeared among the hemorrhoid salve and catarrh curative notices of the *Star-Telegram*. It announced that the Reverend J. Frank Norris would preach Sunday evening on the topic: "Why Dallas Beat Fort Worth in Baseball." A banner proclaiming the meeting and its non-Biblical message was strung over Main Street. His tame Baptists fidgeted. What was Brother Norris up to?

At 7:30 p.m. Sunday, Norris stepped into his pulpit and confronted a packed auditorium. Most in the audience were curiosity seekers. They looked on the skinny Ichabod figure who seemed weak and lifeless in the pulpit and heard his first quiet words: "Dallas beat Fort Worth because Dallas was better prepared. Boys, you had better get prepared for this game of life."

Then without warning, J. Frank Norris attacked. He shouted, wept, exhorted, pulled away his tie and celluloid collar, threw off his suit jacket, ran about the church, up and down aisles. He seared the walls with the warning of judgment, the horrors of hell, and at least one witness claimed to have smelled sulphur, actually felt the heat of Hades. For two hours, Norris ranted his hardshell Baptist message, ending the performance with fists raised, shouting, "Old Devil, you think you've got these boys tonight. But, oh, Devil, you haven't!! You haven't!! These boys are going to knock a home run for Jesus Christ tonight." He sprang into an aisle, bellowing, "Come on, boys, knock a home run for Jesus!" Weeping men and women, panicked by the apparent consequences of their sinfulness, rushed forward for salvation, sliding for home. Sixty lost souls were saved that evening, not the least of which was one belonging to J. Frank Norris. The First Baptist Church never again was a calm garden of worship.

For Norris' stunned conservative congregation, the mutant metamorphosis was incredulous, even insane, and the sight of their God-inflamed Ichabod racing about the church hitting home runs for Jesus must have seemed the behavior of a madman. Exactly why Norris transformed himself from a staid, domesticated Baptist pastor into a hellfire and damnation revivalist, a skinny thunderbolt fired by a vengeful God, will never be known. Perhaps he grew tired of waiting for the Lord to act on his behalf. He wrote only that he decided to turn from "my . . . dead, dull, dry method" and become a "sensationalist." That summer of 1911 Norris' sensationalist preacher act became so popular services moved outside to accommodate the large audiences. As many as one hundred persons weekly joined the church, most of them the uneducated, the poor, the ignorant for whom religion was an emotional anesthetic, for whom the heaven promised by Norris represented a happiness they would never find on earth. The socially prominent congregation looked on its new brothers and sisters in Christ, sniffed indignantly, and began grumbling loudly.

Norris' messages, then and for the remainder of his career, were not from a God of love but one with a terrible swift sword for the wicked, and, he warned endlessly, all of mankind is just naturally, innately sinful. His Bible was The Word, absolute bedrock Truth, each canon, comma and ampersand. He preached Salvation, Rebirth and Immortality, and woe to the unbelievers and instruments of the devil. He was eloquent and loquacious and earthy, so emotional he cried at the drop of a psalm, so animated his frail arms seemed to one observer as "scythes cutting weeds for hell." By autumn the church roll numbered nine hundred members. The old congregation was a minority.

Norris openly defied his original flock. He brought in hundreds of poor people "and gave them free entertainment. Ice cream was served and they got it all over that fine heavy carpet." Next day he received the wrath of the "diamond be-decked sisters of the Ladies Aid" complaining of the pastor's use of their church. Ultimately, he "adjourned all church so-cieties *sine die*, to meet no more" because he was asked to read their announcements in services. His board chairman suggested a sermon topic and Norris told him, "Brother Deacon, your ticket has expired, and when the train slows down at the next water tank you will have your luggage ready to get off."

"You are a damned fool," the chairman replied, accord-ing to Norris, "and this is to notify you that you are fired."

"No," said Norris, "you are the one who is fired."

"The pastor," he later wrote, suggesting he was against syntax as well as sin, "had about as much to say as to how the church should be run as a weaned yearling calf tied to a stob on the outside of a cow lot looking through the cracks of a new gate wanting to be where he is not."

Norris took the fight to the congregation and his new converts, outnumbering the old sheep, presented him with a vote of confidence. He had captured the church.

His pulpit secure, Norris looked outside, to Fort Worth and its sinful ways, to the still-burgeoning Hell's Half Acre, to the countless saloons, to the Godless Sunday picture shows, to the limitless evils of Cowtown. He looked, and smiled. Easy pickings.

J. Frank Norris is a substantial character in the South's fundamental religious history. In a region famed for snake handlers and holy rollers, the fanatical and the outrageous, Norris was for forty years the grandest show of all. He was a superb performer in the pulpit. His sermons encompassed all the passions and emotions of the highly volatile fundamentalist dogma but too they toured the whole of human experience from thumbsucking to black-eyed pea recipes, all presented with a theatrical genius. During Prohibition he raved against bootlegging, Texas' third oldest profession, and regularly dispatched agents to buy moonshine in fruit jars. He stacked the jars around his pulpit and as he spoke against the evils of booze, he smashed each jug in a galvanized tub. The gurgling noisy drama was so popular he repeated the scene many times and a local bootlegger offered to sell him liquor on a regular basis for breakage. When evolution was a topical sin among fundamentalists, Norris paraded monkeys through the church, representing them as Darwin's cousins. For money raising projects he strung rows of clothes lines throughout the church and locked the doors. He would allow the people to leave only when money was fluttering from each clothes pin. Once, for attention, he filled another number two washtub with rattlesnakes for his fascinated audience.

"Wasn't that silly?" his son asked.

"No," said Norris, "I wanted a large audience."

Norris was the most entertaining spectacle in town, better even than the two-reelers and kootch shows against which he railed, and spectators came in droves. By the early 1920s membership of the First Baptist Church reached twelve thousand and the five thousand member Sunday School was, boasted Norris, the world's largest. There was a fundamental Bible college and an association of world-wide fundamentalist churches with total membership of over three thousand. Norris published his own newspaper and established a radio station, KFQB. He became pastor of Temple Baptist Church in Detroit and kept his post in Fort Worth, proclaiming himself spiritual leader of two churches eighteen hundred miles apart.

From the mid-1930s Norris considered himself a world religious figure. He traveled extensively, staging revivals in Ireland, France, Iraq, Iran, Egypt, Scotland and Germany. He met with Churchill and Roosevelt, built churches in Israel and Shanghai.

Norris was the first Protestant minister granted private

audience with a pope. He and Pius XII met and spoke of world events and afterward the Pope, through interpreters, asked permission to pray for the Baptist. Pius XII prayed, then Norris said, "Your eminence, as we say in Texas, I'd like to lay one on you, too."

The interpreters pondered and puzzled over this strange request and asked Norris to repeat his words. Finally they understood and Norris prayed loudly for Pius XII. Departing, the Pope said, "May God bless you."

Norris smiled, and replied, "May God bless you, too."

That J. Frank Norris was allowed even to enter the Vatican was a testimony to the ecumenism of a new era. For thirty years of his inflammable ministry, Catholic degradation was a favorite sermon topic and Godless popery central to Norris' Duke's Mixture of evil "isms"—Catholicism, modernism, socialism, evolutionism, communism. Sin of every stripe was very popular with Brother Norris, holding as he did the standard fundamentalist belief that anyone having a good time was ripe for hell.

Amon Carter, who always had a good time, hated J. Frank Norris, and the publisher's enmity of Norris was the majority position in Fort Worth.

Amon despised the minister not for his religious views, for the publisher had few, but because Norris' notoriety damaged Carter's evangelism of boosterism for Fort Worth. He was "against the unfavorable advertising Fort Worth is receiving from Dr. Norris." Amon couldn't abide a smart aleck.

In that first summer of transformation, Norris began rummaging through Fort Worth's social sinning closets and by autumn of 1911 tar-and-feather talk was in the air. First, Norris led a fight for enforcement of a state law banning all Sunday entertainment and pressured law officials into arresting several picture show projectionists. Next he jumped on liquor and kicked around the saloons. Then he spied the venerable Hell's Half Acre and fell on that sinful eden with the enthusiasm of a prospector finding the mother lode. At Norris' insistence the ministers' association hired a private detective to investigate the Acre. The man reported eighty houses of prostitution and handed over a list of property owners. Eight of the whorehouse landlords were socially and financially prominent in Fort Worth. At least one was a church deacon. Other ministers gulped and dropped the entire matter. Norris smiled. "If a preacher is not stirring up the devil," he said, "he is dead, already sold out."

Norris poked the devil. He read the eight names from his pulpit. He frayed the men's reputation and coupled the tirade with an harangue against city officials who, he shouted, had joined in a conspiracy of sin with Acre prostitutes, thieves and bootleggers. Outside his church, the sermon was not well received.

Amon pointedly told Dr. T. L. Ray, one of Norris' new deacons, that "I wish the church would get Dr. Norris a good job somewhere else."

The controversy simmered for a month, then Norris printed in the weekly *X-Ray* a condemnation of Winfield Scott, Fort Worth's largest property owner and one of the now-infamous Acre Eight.

As winter arrived, animosity for Norris was rife. January 8, the *Star-Telegram* carried an announcement. Mayor W. B. Davis would speak Wednesday at eight o'clock in city hall. His topic: "Liars in Capital Letters." "It is rumored," said the story, "that short and ugly terms will be applied to a number of recent utterances." No women or children admitted.

Davis stood before an overflow crowd and immediately began to verbally lash the hide off J. Frank Norris, ". . . the fanatical outcast."

Norris, opined Davis, was not "worth killing with a dollar ninety-eight cent pistol."

He concluded, "This is a time for heads of homes to act and not a time for sissy boys. If there are fifty red-blooded men in this town, a preacher will be hanging from a lamp post before daylight."

Norris survived the night, but trouble was coming. Two days afterwards, fire broke out in the First Baptist Church auditorium. There was little damage. Firemen suspected arson. Three nights later, Norris sat alone in his church study, preparing a sermon. Two shots were fired through a window. Both missed. January 25, Norris preached on "Things That Have Happened in Fort Worth in the Last Thirty Days." Once again, he condemned corrupt city officials.

At 2:30 a.m., February 4, a freezing watchman heard an explosion, then saw flames rising from the fortress-like First Baptist Church. He fired his pistol three times as an alarm. At the same time, five blocks away at Norris' home, burning oil rags were tossed onto the back porch. By dawn, Fort Worth's most ornate church was blackened rubble. The fire at Norris' home caused minor damage.

The following day Amon, president of the Fort Worth Board of Trade, announced that five thousand dollars "would be paid for capture of the incendiaries." The reward, he said, was "to correct reports that Fort Worth is in the hands of lawless elements."

Norris was elated by the events. He moved services to a theater and remounted his attack. His enemies' persecution of him was "an attack on righteousness," and he proclaimed, "If anybody thinks a bunch of these machine . . . politicians can make a fight on my wife's husband, and I will do as a flop-eared, pot-licker, suck-egg hound, when he tucks his tail between his legs and runs down tin can alley—well, they have another think comin.'"

March 2, fire heavily damaged Norris' home. The family escaped by leaping from a second floor window. Ten days after the fire Norris was indicted for perjury, and a week later, he also was charged with arson.

The April trial was a sensation, its popularity undiminished even when reports had to compete with newspaper space on the *Titanic*'s sinking. Norris appeared each day with his hands folded around a worn Bible. Baptist church members crowded the courtroom while outside young boys distributed religious tracts. Church ladies held afternoon prayer sessions.

Prosecution tactics centered on two threatening notes Norris claimed had been sent him and a deacon, G. H. Connell; Norris' note warned, "You have escaped so far, but look

out. The end is not yet; there is something more coming."
Connell's letter was more revealing. It read, "I and others
have tried to warn that damb [sic] preacher of yours—he
continues to slander the best men in town. We have the dope
on him where he was caught with a woman from Fort Worth
in a St. Louis Hotel last year. How can you keep such a man
when the above is known all over town? If he remains the
proof will be coming." Neither note was signed.

The prosecution showed that a torn piece of stationery
found in Norris' home after the February 4 fire matched the
jagged edges of the note allegedly received by the pastor.
Warren Andrews, a bank clerk brought in as a handwriting
expert, testified that a sample of Norris' writing was the same
as in both letters and, too, the minister misspelled "damn"
as "damb."

That Sunday Norris spoke on martyrdom, of, as it happened, Jesus, not himself, but the analogy was clear and not
lost on the largest crowd ever to hear him preach. A rumor
circulated he would be shot in the pulpit and the curious
came the same way people go to auto races, expecting wrecks.

April 11, the prosecution played its trump, Mrs. K. K.
Taylor, former financial secretary of Norris' church. Mrs.
Taylor's testimony stunned spectators. That winter, she said,
Norris came to her home fretting that his congregation was
"not doing enough for the Kingdom." "Unless a great calam-
ity comes," she quoted Norris as saying, "I fear the church
will never do its duty."

The pastor, she said, wanted a new five or six-story
church. Norris also cussed his enemies, using "that name no
man wants his mother's name associated with."

After the church burned, Norris returned to her home,
sat on a sofa, slapped his knee and laughed, "Well, I got
Teddy [Roosevelt] beat. Teddy never had two extras out about
him in less than 12 hours."

Norris asked her to mail several letters for him. She refused, and the pastor left. Distressed, she prayed all night,
then took her story to the prosecutor.

Strong stuff. The prosecution felt confident. It should not

have. A week later, the jury voted once and found Norris innocent of all charges. The courtroom exploded in Baptist joy. Men cheered, women wept. Norris smiled. "A black mammy," said the *Star-Telegram*, waved her finger in Judge Tom Simmons' face and said, "Woe be unto you." Spontaneously, the crowd began singing, "Nearer My God to Thee." Non-Baptists gnashed their teeth in anger.

Thus vindicated—Christianity really was on trial, he claimed—J. Frank Norris began searching for more causes with which to sensationalize his burgeoning ministry. More and more as his church grew, Norris isolated his people by preaching they and they alone were chosen by God to smite a sinful world. He, Norris lectured his flock, was a "Saint of God" and his trial was like Luther in front of the Diet of Worms and "As Paul before Agrippa." As a persecuted saint, Norris preached that he bore "the cross of Christ to the reproach of the world." "The Powers of Darkness" were threatening the church, "his" church since Norris held deed on the new building.

Norris' enemies grew in numbers as large as his power and influence. "The Lord must love enemies," said a contemporary, "because he made so many for J. Frank Norris." Brother Norris was a hard man to like.

He proselytized among other churches, including Baptist, by charging their pastors had "sold out to the forces of compromise, modernism and decay." "Modernists cuckooed the Methodists and Congregationalists," he preached. When other pastors complained, he called them "little two by four simian-headed sentimentalists."

Not surprisingly, the Fort Worth ministers' association expelled him.

Unperturbed, Norris next dumped all Southern Baptist Sunday school literature as "junk." He claimed Southern Baptists had made "papal demands" to him. When evolution became a heated topic, he found the Godless philosophy lurking in his alma mater, and preached against the "apes and monkeys of Baylor University." Baylor students hanged Norris in effigy.

The Texas Baptist Convention expelled him and Southern Baptists finally shed themselves of the pesky preacher. He claimed he was in the right and they wanted to still his voice. Actually, they just wanted to shut him up.

Alone to head his own church organization, Norris began gathering other fundamentalist churches into the fold, while continuing to kick at stately Baptist kneecaps with all that he commanded—tracts, booklets, resolutions, airwaves, and lungs.

During the early 1920s, when hatred of J. Frank Norris was as popular as bootleg whiskey, Dr. L. P. Scarborough, president of the Southwestern Baptist Theological Seminary, distributed 100,000 tracts on "Norrisism." And prominent Baptists bought seven consecutive nights of radio time to condemn Norris. He was called malicious, perjurer, liar, thief, scoundrel, despicable, damnable, criminal, wicked, corrupt and hellish. Norris, ever the showman, was delighted. He purchased newspaper space to advertise the attacks on him and bought radio time immediately after each Baptist broadcast. As they signed off, he signed on. Norris asked the listening audience to forgive those "high priests of Baptists." J. Frank Norris never turned the other cheek.

Amon continued to despise Norris and what he imagined the preacher's publicity was doing to Fort Worth's reputation. Sometime before 1920 Norris called on Carter in the publisher's office and suggested the two men declare a truce. They should join forces to run Fort Worth. Amon cussed the pastor and ordered him out.

And the *Record* declared editorially: "We will not again publish the name of J. Frank Norris in these columns."

In middle age Frank Norris was a handsome man with graying hair, a firm chin, overly large ears, thin esthetic lips and those brooding eyes. His priorities shifted from Baptist-baiting to other more secular matters. His stature was such that William Jennings Bryan asked him to testify for the prosecution in the Scopes trial but the judge ruled no Biblical experts could be heard. He briefly flirted with the Ku Klux Klan as the Fort Worth chapter's official religious spokesman, then during the plague of Prohibition merrily began kicking around Catholics.

He associated the growth of bootlegging with Catholicism and preached on the topics, "Shall Catholics and Bootleggers Elect the Next U.S. Senate?" and "Shall Roman Catholics Rule Tarrant County Today?" Norris again was fishing into local political waters, defining the 1926 city administration as "morally corrupt" because Mayor H. C. Meacham was a man "with known Roman Catholic associations." That Catholic mafia syndrome occupied Norris' pulpit ideas and even when he campaigned to have Fort Worth streets and alleys cleaned of trash the versatile pastor was able to associate the garbage can crusade with papal lust. He denounced the Catholic puppet, Meacham, in his church and printed 62,000 copies of the sermon for distribution. Boys were posted around Meacham's department store to hand out the pamphlets to each customer.

Meacham was furious. He fired six employees, all members of Norris' congregation. The martyred six became a sermon topic in which Norris pled with God to punish the "dishonest" Meacham. The message was printed and Norris' boys once again surrounded the mayor's store. The preacher announced he would discuss Meacham and official graft the following Sunday.

July 17, 1926 was a scorching Saturday and the afternoon heat drove *Star-Telegram* reporters to the only logical retreat in Prohibition-dry Fort Worth—a bar hidden in an old house three blocks west of the newspaper office. The editorial department held a skeleton crew. James Record was there, and DeWitt Reddick, a part-time schoolboy reporter. They heard a noise. Both looked up.

The dignified Jimmy North was skipping down the hall, his arm raised for attention, shouting, "J. Frank Norris just shot and killed a man. . . . HOORAY!"

Without credible witnesses no one who ever knew the gentle, kindly North would believe him capable of cheering the tragedy, but his spontaneous outburst was testimony to the deeply-felt acrimony Norris created in Fort Worth. Nei-

ther North nor Record would have allowed their religious beliefs to infringe on *Star-Telegram* readers, nor would they
permit any but the most correct criticism of Norris to appear
in editorial columns, but both hoped the tragic shooting
would be the means of at long last silencing the vitriolic
Norris. Within hours most of Fort Worth shared that hope.

Norris shot D. E. Chipps, a lumber yard owner and close
friend of Meacham who, according to others, was "a drunkard and a bully." In Norris' version of the shooting, Chipps
telephoned him and demanded the preacher stop his crusade
against Meacham. Norris said Chipps threatened to kill him.
He borrowed a pistol from the church janitor and secreted it
in a desk drawer. Twenty minutes later Chipps—arriving
straight from Meacham's office—burst into Norris' church
study and confronted the pastor.

"I am going to kill you for what you said in your sermon,
damn you," Norris quoted Chipps as yelling. Chipps moved
his right hand to a back pocket. Norris opened the desk
drawer, grabbed the pistol and shot Chipps three times.

Chipps was unarmed.

Eighteen days later a grand jury indicted Norris for murder and the district attorney announced he would seek the
death penalty.

Norris' version was partially substantiated by L. H. Nutt,
an accountant and devout member of the First Baptist Church
congregation. Nutt was in the study but out of the lumber-
man's vision. He testified that Chipps reached for his back
pocket in a threatening gesture while cursing Norris. A second witness arrived moments afterwards. Norris was rushing
out of the study. "I have killed me a man," the witness said
Norris boasted.

Open gossip among church members held that Meacham
sent Chipps to kill Norris. The rumors were printed in Los
Angeles and Chicago newspapers and Meacham threatened
suit. He claimed Chipps had visited him 30 minutes before
the shooting to solicit a donation for a painting of Amon
Carter which was to be placed in the Fort Worth Club.

Chipps, theorized Meacham, undoubtedly was in Norris'

office to ask for a donation. Chipps only was reaching into his rear pocket for a donor's list when Norris shot him without provocation.

The trial was moved to Austin, set for January 1927, and as it opened reporters invaded the city to cover what they believed would be the end of J. Frank Norris. Every hotel and boarding house room in town was filled. The courtroom was so crowded witnesses had to enter through an open window.

The *Star-Telegram* provided an unusual service for its readers.

Jim Record, two reporters and two court stenographers were in the courtroom. The stenographers recorded every word uttered by witnesses, lawyers and the judge. Record edited the copy and it was sent via two leased wires to Fort Worth. The verbatim testimony, which covered as much as seven and one-half full newspaper pages and never less than four open pages, totaled almost half-a-million words.

Amon Carter said the word-for-word reporting and unusually large space devoted to the trial was a record, and perhaps it was. The approach to trial reporting was at least unique in American journalism.

Fort Worth was convinced Norris was guilty of murder, guilty of killing an unarmed man. Only the pastor's hard-shelled flock seemed to believe him innocent. And the jury. The jury needed just one unanimous vote to free Norris as a man only protecting his life. "May god pity and forgive them," Norris told reporters, after the courtroom exploded into loud thankful prayers and hymn-singing. "I stand on Romans 8:28. . . ."

Later in life Norris would tell his son of the tragedy. "I shot him like I would a dog in the night who threatened my family," the pastor declared.

Immediately after the verdict of innocence, Norris went home to Fort Worth, to his church where, he later wrote, "The station was thronged with the multitudes . . . streets were lined with crowds from there to the church. Regardless of the bitter cold night . . . the great auditorium was packed to standing room and multitudes turned away."

J. Frank Norris was back in the fold, safe amid his fundamentalist Baptists who believed the infamous preacher was a true saint of God. Two years later the church was burned to the ground for the third and final time.

WIMPY TORTILLA ROLLER

1972
THE LOST ART OF
TORTILLA ROLLING

It has come to my attention that tortilla rolling has slipped. The art is not what it used to be.

Very few of us can properly handle a tortilla any more. It takes deft hands and a certain flair for showmanship and a dedication to craftsmanship and an appreciation for the ambrosia of Mexican food.

The staff of life that is a correctly prepared tube of tortillas and frijoles is the essence of elegant dining and should not be undertaken in a slap-hazard manner, yet there are those who do so through ignorance or laziness and it is a sad, sad thing to see.

Crude, crude. Nobody cares about public manners anymore.

The state of the art is such that I often am ashamed to sit down to a plate of enchiladas, tacos, rice, frijoles and tortillas. Why, I have even seen uncouth eaters who actually folded a tortilla.

That shows you how far down some diners have come. They are to be pitied, of course, but that does not excuse their bad manners.

Just why tortilla rolling is in such a sad state, I don't know. I can guess. For one thing Texas has taken in a lot of outsiders in the last few years, people who simply don't understand tortillas or don't care how they act in public. Probably their friends are too embarrassed to correct the newcomers' tortilla conduct.

And parents seem not to mind the ignorance of their

children. Sure, they'll speak to them about sex education but I'll bet not one parent in a thousand brings up the subject of tortillas. There's nothing wrong with mixing sex and tortillas.

Schools disregard the tortilla. Students are taught to tear down a car engine or operate a computer or square a root but teachers sidestep the craft of tortilla rolling.

The lack of tortilla-rolling expertise, too, must fall in with the general decline of pride in craftmanship.

Perhaps an explanation of tortilla rolling is necessary. Pay attention, please. Here are the basics:

A tortilla is a flat, thin round food. It and frijoles—which are beans cooked, mashed and refried—are elementary pieces of that body of comestibles known as Mexican food.

Chicanos passed the tortilla on to the rest of us. Mexican-Americans know how to treat tortillas and frijoles. They are born to it, and they probably are ashamed of our improper use.

There are two kinds of tortillas. Corn and flour. Flour tortillas are late-comers and were innovated in San Antonio during the last century. The corn tortilla runs back to the Aztecs, and Cortez's soldiers ate them more than 500 years ago.

A tortilla is made by grinding corn, adding a little lime juice and water; then it is flattened and fried. Because it is of classic design—a circle—the tortilla is perfect for rolling. Here is how to do it:

Place a warm tortilla in the left hand with your palm cupped slightly to form a trough. Spoon in at least two ounces of frijoles. Press very gently to spread the frijoles (the beans should not be nearer than one-half inch from the tortilla border).

Now comes the delicate part. With the right hand, lay over that edge of the tortilla nearest you (watch it, don't mash the frijoles again). Now, with the first three fingers of the right hand carefully roll the edge forward until you have formed a tortilla tube.

With practice the rolling of tortillas can become an accomplished art and done with a skilled, fluid motion is an amazing thing to see.

There are variations on the basic performance (and ingredients) and while I cannot argue with individual tastes I prefer to stick with the basics.

Some like butter spread on a tortilla and others will add a dash of salt. There are those who include rice with the frijoles. But that seems too lumpy for me.

A word on the flour tortilla. It is not a perfect tortilla, only a copy, and while it will do in emergencies, I'll go with the original corn version every time. For one thing, a flour tortilla will break if not cooked properly (and I always send flour tortillas that break back to the chef just as I would a poor bottle of wine).

Watching an old tortilla-rolling hand at work is a thing of beauty. I saw one the other day at Joe Garcia's. He selected a hot tortilla. With a snap of the wrist he flipped the tortilla. It made one turn and landed softly on his palm, (real showmanship). His other hand, in the meantime, had readied the frijoles.

He applied the beans, there was a blur of moving fingers and, presto, a perfectly prepared tortilla.

Now, there was a tortilla roller. It's good to know there are a few of the old masters still around.

1971

COWTOWN CULTURE

Opera, I have learned, is not as bad as it sounds. An Old Master is as companionable as, say, Old Charter. A ballerina *sur les pointes* has as much grace as a bird dog spotting quail, and considerably more sex appeal.

Culture, though, is an abominable term. Too pompous and snooty. Mention culture to a guy who buys his beer at the corner grocery and he slouches lower in his chair, sighing for lost causes.

By its most base interpretation culture can be a three-bank shot in the corner pocket or a hot grounder between the legs of a 10-year-old sandlot shortstop. Ulysses is no less a noble character than Uncle Remus. The baton of Leonard Bernstein presides over music equally as important as that caused by Boots Randolph.

Art produces a cultural overkill. But to be art it must function at two levels—(1) the fustian stage of ethereal perception and (2) the Eyeball-Ear Drum Test—that is, if it catches your eye or ear and you like it, that's art.

An apocryphal story explains this culture gap. It is said to have happened in the Amon Carter Museum. A West Texas rancher, one of those who fill Fort Worth each January for its stock show and rodeo, halted to inspect a Remington painting. The picture showed a buffalo kill by a Plains Indian. The Indian rode a spirited horse. Peering closely, the old rancher crinkled his eyes and grinned.

Nearby stood one of those prototypical *grande dames* of the arts. She peeked over the West Texan's shoulder and gushed, "Ah! The Noble Savage."

The rancher eyed her coolly. "I wouldn't know about that ma'am," he said, "but he's riding a dang good horse."

I suspect Fred Remington would have cheered the rancher's appraisal of his painting. He and that other western wanderer, Charles Russell, were earthy guys. Each is represented in the Amon Carter Museum with paintings and sculpture, important because the collection chronologically tracks their odyssey across the American West.

The museum—it is much more than an elegant repository of art—is America's foremost western authority. Scholars revere it. Teachers lose themselves in its archives. But the value to Fort Worth is that the entanglement of culture levels is met and conquered in this rugged building faced with Texas shell limestone.

Amon Carter's museum sits in Fort Worth's cultural center. The center has an official name, Carter Square, which appears in few more places than City Council minutes. Once the Chamber of Commerce took to calling it the Acropolis of the Southwest. Plain folks say they are "going out to Will Rogers," meaning the auditorium-coliseum-tower complex named for the Oklahoma humorist.

Whatever it is called, it has 85 acres filled with arty things. There are 20 buildings covering 35 acres, and among them four museums and three theaters.

Culture lovers—whatever those are—come in the form of children hiking through the Museum of Science and History or enrolled in any of dozens of classes offered by the museum, members of the Fort Worth Art Museum Association, or just people who walk in to look at a painting or sculpture or attend a play in Scott Theater or a summer musical at Casa Manana. Too, more than a half-a-million people show up for the Southwestern Exposition and Fat Stock Show and Rodeo (many of those buildings are stock barns). And it is presumed many of the art lovers are the same gentle persons who scream for blood at hockey games in the coliseum.

While Fort Worth seems to appreciate its museum and art stuff, outside recognition is frequent. In late 1971 the Amon Carter Museum and the Museum of Science and History were two among the first 16 museums in the United States to be accredited by the American Association of Museums.

No other museums in the Southwest were chosen and New York was the only other city with two museums on the select list. That's two Fort Worth museums of 425 inspected by the association committee.

[Since then, a new temple of enlightenment, the Kimbell Museum, has opened. Fort Worthers can inspect the works of European Renaissance artists before walking over to the hockey game. That is the way of things here.]

The elite museums, however, cannot become too peacockish. It is difficult to peer down one's nose at a three-breasted Picasso while pig-judging is held across the parking lot. That, for me, is the center's elementary attraction. It is a Culture-for-Everyman place in which diversions range from Cole Porter to cole slaw, Bach to broncos, Beethoven to basketball, ice skating to isometrics.

Fort Worth is not the first city to have a culture center for esthetic and pleasurable pastimes. The Acropolis of Athens preceded by several thousand years. But it may be the first in which you can milk a cow and view a Renoir-sketched milkmaid without questioning the paradox.

As with others the Acropolis occupies a hill, lying west from downtown across the city's vermicular and dowdy river, the Trinity.

The center is at once reflective of, and in conflict with, Fort Worth's public image. The city began as an army frontier camp (the bald truth is it never was a fort and early city fathers lied a little about their town's status). Supposedly the camp was to serve as protection for settlers but that was a waste of time and men. Local Indians ignored the post. Try as they did the soldiers could not provoke the Indians into attack, and Fort Worth passed into history without a single redskin uprising to grace its name.

Cattle, though, did what Lipan Comanches could not. Longhorns gave Fort Worth a reputation. Not all good, mind you, but saloon keepers liked it. The famed Texas cattle trails north to Kansas passed near Fort Worth, and trail hands enjoyed going to town to fight and drink and such.

Those cowboys camped near the quiet hill above the Trinity, not caring about coming culture. Art meant little to them. Probably they could not have distinguished between a contralto and a chippie. Art for them was the inevitable painting of a reclining nude hanging above the bar, of which were more than a few. If a song was heard it came from lips of a plump bargirl who had other duties in the backroom. The only acting in town was done over poker tables.

In that cattle time Fort Worth's reputation for base pleasures was enormous and attracted the West's characters. Buffalo Bill and his girl friend drank in the White Elephant Saloon. Luke Short, a fast gunhand who wore a stovepipe hat, and Doc Holliday, already consumptive, chummed around. Temple Houston, youngest son of old Sam, came to town often, usually wearing a rattlesnake for a hatband. Sam Bass bought all of his bank and train robbing supplies in Fort Worth.

These baddies eventually left but of course culture did not chase them away. They left behind thriving cattle—Fort Worth's stockyards still are immense—and butcher industries. The city became a rail center (to move all of those cows, both mooing and skinned). West Texans struck oil and migrated to Fort Worth to spend their wealth. Their children still are spending it.

Fort Worth happend upon the twentieth century as a town with the ambrosia of the west on its breath.

Fort Worth is best approached from the west with a late afternoon sun at your back. U.S. Highway 377 arrives from that direction and is laid across the mild hills which give the land form. It is distant country, a place for seeing horizons, not the flat lean land of far West Texas but a prairie and one that has changed little in context for more than 100 years.

Much of western America must have been as this, before man and before the absolute finality of progress. It is a nostalgic land. In the afternoon sun, the earth and grasses, beige for summers, absorb light's yellow tones, and they are as in Spanish Andalusia, a rich, yet soft, lemon-colored plain. In a few pastures are white-faced cattle, the aristocrats of ranching country. And windmills, the west's clanking sentinels, stand for sunsets. It is this grassy plain, between oak thickets of Texas' Cross Timbers section and the delta-flat pinelands east of Dallas, that establishes Fort Worth's mood.

No one ever will write sonnets to the city or essay its esthetics but Fort Worth is a city with which to be comfortable.

Progress has caused Fort Worth to be tied to Dallas and neither city particularly is happy about it. That hyphen is at best a yoke for the two cities. The jim-dash functions as a coupling device for joint projects, such as the huge supersonic airport between Dallas/Fort Worth, or Fort Worth/Dallas as we say at this end.

Beneath that hyphen are a dozen towns which bear the common title, "Mid-Cities Area." Arlington seems about to burst out. It has Six Flags Over Texas, the state's single most popular visitor attraction, and the Texas Rangers, a professional baseball team that formerly played under the name, Washington Senators. Nearby, at Grand Prairie, Lion Country Safari is an animal preserve through which visitors may drive.

That hyphen has not married twins. Dallas is bigger, wealthier and has more industrial muscle. It is champagne cocktails at midnight and diamonds on the half-shell. Because Fort Worth is on the cusp of cattle country it is a western place. (Despite a Chamber of Commerce's effort once to hide its agrarian stain by calling it "The Now Town," a cutesy play on Fort Worth's long-borne nickname, "Cowtown.")

Fort Worth has a folksy personality which if transposed to human mannerisms would cause it to drawl, blush and scuff its toe in the dirt. More yep than yes the city's voice would be laconic, its words colloquial. Hollywood has made millions with this character. He is hero to men, patient with children, lovingly polite and gentle for women.

It is a most difficult chore to play sophisticate when a mayor wears boots for ground-breaking ceremonies or bankers come to work in Stetsons. In downtown Fort Worth the city kindly has left untouched a long brick-topped street, one of the few remaining in the country. All others have been resurfaced with smoother materials. The brick street (and there are several shorter ones outside downtown) are reflective of

times past. North, stockyards stand beside meat-packing plants and a rail switching complex. Exchange Avenue, once the Texas cowboy center, is false-fronted to mirror that cattle image.

Fort Worth has been described as a village that just happens to have almost half-a-million population. This village syndrome comes, I think, from people who moved here from small West Texas towns where the talk and pace are slow. They brought the grace of small towns with them. All of this shows up on weekends when the people fill city parks, crowd through the zoo (*Life* Magazine once called it one of the half-dozen best zoos in the country), and hike into the Botanical Garden.

COWTOWN CULTURE • 101

And they swarm all over the Acropolis, acting as though it is not a culture place filled with arty stuff. What the center has come to be is a good deal. But it is an accident, albeit an auspicious one. Dallas, naturally, caused its beginning. Or rather Fort Worth's always-competitive reaction to Dallas is the reason.

The time was 1936, and Texas staged its centennial. Dallas was given the official celebration. Fort Worth decided to have its own—uncertified—Texas birthday party. They called it Frontier Fiesta. Using a mixture of local and federal funds the city built the auditorium-coliseum-tower complex, plus various out-buildings on the then-vacant hill.

There was a rodeo under the coliseum dome and a wild west show, a saloon with a polished bar on which danced six 200-pound dollies, Casa Manana (forerunner of the aluminum-skinned theater-in-the-round now fixed in the center), a circus and beauty contests.

The Texas Sweetheart Pageant was won by Faye Cotton, a dark-haired restaurant cashier from Borger in the Texas Panhandle. Miss Cotton was so excited by being selected over 75 other contestants that she immediately went out and had a tonsillectomy.

No one seemed to miss the curvy Faye Cotton because there was another girl hanging around. Sally Rand. And her Nude Ranch Revue.

It is to Sally—and there are those who will lament the source—Fort Worth owes its reputation as a place of *haute culture*.

Sally adequately bulged eyeballs there on the hill. Her costume—her only costume—was a handful of feathers. The blonde slip of a girl flitted around the stage several times daily doing what she must have considered a form of ballet.

Behind her, blaring through loud speakers, was the first authentic classical music performed on ground that was to become the Acropolis of the Southwest.

A melange of Beethoven, Brahms and Debussy. Sally's stripping music.

Thanks, Sally, for everything.

1983

TEXAS CUISINE

There is a major error in this story on Texas foods. Chicken fried steak, I have since learned, did not originate with Jimmy Don Perkins in Lamesa, Texas. Jimmy Don and the chicken fried steak legend are a fiction invented by an Austin writer more than a decade ago. The essentials of his tall story, however, have entered Texas mythology and are now accepted as fact, even in the Lone Star Book of Records. I am pleased to do my part in expanding the legend. A good lie deserves all the circulation it can get.

Of the world's four great cuisines—French, Chinese, Italian and Texan—only the last-named requires a single knife and fork. The others insist on multiple silverware and crystal goblets, linen napkins and a guy who does nothing but pour Lafite-Rothschild '69.

With Texas food you get one knife and one fork, a plastic iced-tea glass, paper napkins and a waitress who calls you "Honey" and believes a sommelier is somebody who races an eight-cylinder Sommel with overhead cams at the local drag strip.

This simplicity of hardware and mechanics is consistent with the philosophy of dining on Texas cuisine. Less is better, quicker and cheaper. Texas cuisine is pure and uncomplex, bedrock basic, and serving it with two knives, three forks and a silver gravy boat only blurs the senses and taints the ambience of a momentous dining experience.

Texas foods, jazz and jeans are the only true original American art forms. We're not talking plain American food here, like french fries and pizza, pot roast, Big Macs or tuna fish salad. This is Texas food, authentic Texas cuisine created and developed entirely within the Lone Star State. Accept no substitutes.

In the beginning, genuine Texas food was hardscrabble rations—peasant stuff, born from a land of severe and unforgiving harshness. Whatever grew here, from the tenacious longhorn steer to the weedy African stalk known as okra, fought to live in a region of too little water and too much heat and dust.

Folks ate what they could—the leathery beef, the tasteless thin corncakes cooked by Mexicans, even the cow peas other Southerners fed to their cattle. But what was, of necessity, survival food evolved into a folk art, became a superb, definitive, regional cuisine.

Out of this grand epicurean evolution came some memorable foods: that most succulent of American dishes, chili, and the flour tortilla, on which whole fast-food empires are based, and that magnificent Lucullan feast of the prairie—heavy beef barbecue.

For the record, Texas also invented the ice cream sundae, the Margarita, frozen steak fingers, corn chips, stadium nachos and the Marpeani, which is a regular martini except that the olive is replaced by a blackeyed pea. These, however, are back-burner dishes within the kitchen literature of Texas cuisine and of no immediate interest.

Texas cuisine may be separated into three distinct divisions—barbecue, Mexican food, and that rare and wonderful piece of bucolic fancy, chicken-fried steak. There are subcategories (hamburgers come to mind; only Texas makes real hamburgers) but that trio of foods fills Texas menus and diets and is the heart and soul of Texas cuisine. They are the eternal, essential life-force of Texans, the fuels of our culture and society, because eating out here is a social and sociological occasion, as much gusto as gustatory. You can't "dine out" on Texas foods; that phrase bestows a sophisticated conceit on what are, after all, humble dishes.

Native foods dominate menus in Texas as in no other American region. They are a true cuisine and probably are the last and most enduring of the regional American dishes that developed out of the land and environment. These three major food groups are not just gimmicky dishes trotted out to feed the tourists, like Hawaiian poi and Alabama grits. They are served daily in every town in Texas. We live and die by the chicken-fried steak.

Barbecue is a product of the Texas prairies. Tough long-horn beef was cooked into tenderness over mesquite-wood coals by range-wise chuckwagon chefs. It was the only way that they could make the beef edible. Sauces came later. Today the beef—a prime-cut brisket—has been joined in the barbecue pit by ribs and sausages, all well-lathered with a mouth-watering, dark red sauce, often peppery and always secret. Chili, the fame of which has spread around the world, is the wellspring of our Mexican food, specifically a cooking style that is known as Tex-Mex.

Tex-Mex is an anthropological reality incorporating foods, vivid customs and traditions—even a language—spoken by two million people living along the Mexican border from the Texas Gulf to California. Basically, a Tex-Mex meal consists of enchiladas, tamales, tacos, guacamole, refried beans, spicy rice and hot corn tortillas. (Yes, I know, other states and regions serve Mexican foods like these but it's not Tex-Mex. Latecomers like New Mexico and Arizona insist on smothering Mexican dishes in sour cream—a base, barbaric corruption of good food.)

As splendid and noble as barbecue and Tex-Mex are, both pale before that Great God Beef dish, chicken-fried steak.

No single food better defines the Texas character; it has, in fact, become a kind of nutritive metaphor for the romanticized, prairie-hardened personality of Texans. Chicken-fried steak is the toughest piece of beef, tenderized and civilized and brought to the table as the nucleus of a royal feast, the hub of what nationally syndicated columnist Liz Smith (a Texan) called "a 5,000-calorie meal."

It is never eaten alone but always as the centerpiece for an almost ritualistic *table d'hôte* that is nourishment as much for the soul and spirit as for the body. As with all dishes of Texas cuisine, chicken-fried steak is presented with graceful simplicity. First, the steak, then white cream gravy, potatoes (french fried or baked), a crispy iceberg-lettuce-and-sliced-tomato salad (traditionally, the dressing is creamy French), iced tea and hot biscuits with real butter and perhaps with honey on the side. That format rarely changes no matter where in Texas chicken-fried steak is ordered.

No one knows who developed barbecue and Tex-Mex. They evolved naturally. Chicken-fried steak, however, can be attributed to a single, largely unheralded hero. According to the *Lone Star Book of Records*, Jimmy Don Perkins—that's a magnificent Texas-style name—was a cook in a small cafe in Lamesa, Texas, in 1911 when he misunderstood the order of a customer. Jimmy battered a thin steak and deep-fried it in hot oil. Eureka! Instant immortality, if not fame.

The unfortunate thing about Texas food is that it is the only one of the four great world cuisines that is not transplanted easily. It is possible, for example, to find a decent French meal in Bangkok, but impossible to sit down to a memorable plate of Texas barbecue even in, say, Louisiana, not to mention Warsaw and Toledo (either Spain or Ohio). By and large, Texas cuisine—the real stuff—stops at the border. You must live here, or visit, to experience genuine Texas foods.

Finding barbecue, Tex-Mex and chicken-fried steak in Texas is like looking for stars on a clear night. They're everywhere. Every city, town, village and hamlet with any dollop of pride dishes up one or all of the imperishable trio. Some, admittedly, are better than others.

A recent survey by the Texas Tourist Development Agency found these to be the most recommended Texas cuisine restaurants in the state.

Barbecue: Gaylen's in Arlington, Angelo's in Fort Worth, Sutphen's in Amarillo, Tony Roma's in Dallas, Dozier's in Fulshear, and the Elgin Market in Elgin.

Tex-Mex: Joe T. Garcia's in Fort Worth, Casita Jorge's and Matt's El Rancho in Austin, Chiquita's in Dallas, and Mi Tierra in San Antonio.

Chicken-fried steak: Massey's in Fort Worth, Sutler's in Fort Davis, Hickory Hollow Inn in Houston, Cottonwood Inn in La Grange, the Boondocks west of Port Arthur, and Goodson's Cafe, northeast of Tomball (which is itself northwest of Houston).

There are other restaurants and cafes which serve Texas cuisine of as good or better quality. Many of these establishments are in small towns and are rarely searched out by food reviewers and guide book writers.

My good friend August, who is an East Texas fisherman of some renown, has developed an infallible system for discovering the best Texas cuisine cafes in strange towns. He rates them by the number of pickup trucks that are parked out front.

"Never, never, never stop at a one-pickup cafe," he counsels. "The chicken-fried steak will be one of them frozen, factory-breaded things. The waitress will be a high-school girl who sticks her thumb in the gravy. Everything'll be fixed in a microwave."

A two-pickup cafe is not much better. Three pickups out front assure some basic skill in preparing Texas cuisine. But, four- and five-pickup cafes. . . .

"Stop quick in them places," advises August. "The waitress'll write your order on one of them little green pads with lines on it and the menu is on a chalkboard hanging over the cash register. The coffee'll be hot and fresh and the waitress will bring you more even when you don't ask her for it. And the chicken-fried steak'll be fresh and tender with good sopping gravy and big biscuits with a jar of fresh honey. They'll even have, maybe, homemade pecan pie that they'll heat up and serve with ice cream all over it."

August, a gourmet with maturity and taste, knows his chicken-fried steak. Trust him. He, and the millions of other Texans who daily consume tons of it, cannot be wrong. Chicken-fried steak is a world-class meal.

And for that we thank you, Jimmy Don Perkins, wherever you are.

The Best Little Chicken-Fried
Steak House in Texas

The correct name is Herb Massey's Dinner Place, a stately title befitting Texas' foremost chicken-fried steak joint, and the location is 1805 8th Avenue in Fort Worth.

Nobody I know calls it anything but Massey's. It is a homey place, jammed with Depression-chrome, laminated-top tables and overstuffed red plastic booths.

When Herb Massey opened his restaurant in the late 1940s, he knew what people in Fort Worth liked—chicken-fried steak. And he knew how to cook it better than anyone else. Now, almost four decades later, Massey's is the best known chicken-fried steak restaurant in Texas and son Charles continues to supervise the kitchen from which have been served, more or less, three million plates of Texans' favorite meal.

No real secret to any of this. Every ingredient is bought fresh daily. Every dish is made from scratch. Nothing is prepared in advance. The cook doesn't start until he receives an order. Brillat-Savarin would have approved of Massey's chicken-fried steak.

In its raw state, it is round steak, a tough piece of beef. Massey's buys only the inside cuts of the round (the outside, says Charles, is much tougher "because that's the part the cow lays on"). Massey's stipulates that the meat must be run through a tenderizing machine twice, first in one direction then in another, to thoroughly break down the tough fibers. Correctly tenderized, Massey's chicken-fried steak can be cut with a fork.

Chicken-Fried Steak

Use two pounds of good-grade inside round steak, ½ to ¾ inch thick. Ask butcher to tenderize or pound thoroughly on both sides with meat-tenderizing mallet. Trim off all gristle and fat. Cut into pieces five to six inches in diameter. Flour each piece thoroughly and shake off excess. Dip in batter and drain. Then flour again and shake off excess. Use deep fryer half-filled with a good brand of vegetable cooking oil. Preheat to 325°. Cook meat seven to ten minutes or until golden brown.

Chicken-Fried
Steak Gravy

1 stick margarine
8 cups milk
½ cup vegetable cooking oil
1 cup flour
2 tsp salt

Melt margarine completely. Add milk and mix thoroughly. Bring to a boil. Blend flour into oil, add to heated milk. Stir until smooth and thickened. Remove from heat. Add salt and pepper to taste.

Chicken-Fried
Steak Batter

3 tbs sugar
½ tsp salt
1 whole egg
1 tbs baking powder
2 cups milk

Mix the first four ingredients with half of the milk and stir until smooth. Add remainder of milk and mix well.

Chicken-Fried
Steak Biscuits

2 cups flour
1 tsp salt
3 tsp baking powder
5 tbs butter
¾ cup milk

Sift all the dry ingredients into a bowl. Cut in butter until mixture looks like coarse cornmeal. Add milk and mix until smooth. Knead dough on a floured board, roll and cut biscuits with floured rim of glass. Place biscuits on floured baking sheet and place in preheated oven at 425°. Bake about 12-15 minutes or until brown on top. Makes about 20 biscuits.

1971

AMERICA'S BEST TOURIST TRAP

Ok, it's a tourist trap. I know it. You know it. No sham or shame about that indisputable fact. New Orleans is a tourist trap, an unequivocal, glittering, virtuosic first fiddle hustler of the buck.

Style. That's New Orleans' secret. Style. No cheap chic. No maudlin schmaltz. Forget the pocket change and go straight for the wallet and credit cards. But do it with great dollops of style.

New Orleans sells itself, its baroque history, the tasselated, festooned romantic past, like one of those television hucksters with his vegetonic tomato slicers. Strips you bare, picks you clean, with the French Quarter kitsch, the Garden District's elegant jumble, the streetcars, street artists, Fat City tomfoolery, antiques, the plantation homes, the squishy Southern softness of it all.

New Orleans is a blatant tourist trap, and I like it better each time I visit.

The Quarter—Vieux Carre—centers on Bourbon Street, an adventurous avenue of bar after bar, rock joints, jazz halls, B girls, strippers, T-shirt shops (T-shirts are a growth industry in the French Quarter), adult movie houses. The sidewalk spielers pull at you, yell at you, leering, laughing, daring, promising.

"Our girls are more naked than theirs," declared one, indicating an across-the-street competitor. Intriguing approach, although once total nudity is attained it is a mystery to me how the effect can be improved on.

Bourbon Street is a kind of tacky circus after dark, a carnival of extremes, a sound and light saturnalia. Clarinets sighing blues, trumpets soaring, the harsh thumpings of electric basses, the sing-song of bar spielers. Musicians copping smokes between sets, holding their instruments under their arms. Men in tuxedos, women in ball gowns, coming from some formal affair to slum for awhile. Half-dressed showgirls walking to work at the saloons where they finish undressing. Sweet Emma, whose one-handed piano playing is legendary. Danny Barker, who plays banjo with a verve denying his seventy-plus years. The waiters in Galatoire's who gently insult you while serving the best Trout Marguery in town. Chris Owens, once a girls' basketball team star at Fort Worth's Texas Wesleyan College, now bouncing in her own club. Hirt and Fountain, the Dukes of Dixieland, the Famous Door, voodoo shops and a seafood cafe called Desire. A shrimp bar named Desire? Tennessee Williams, take a note.

A frantic place, Bourbon Street. Yet, move a block away, on Royal street, and the night is calm, quiet, interrupted only by the clop of horse-drawn carriages, the footsteps of strolling couples—Royal Street may be the only place remaining in America where a man can comfortably and contentedly appear in public wearing a plantation-white suit, escorting a lady dressed in organdy. Royal leads to Jackson Square, a mere three centuries old, and, at night, empty of its artists and plastic ashtray hucksters. The levee beside the Mississippi has lost its Grey Line tourists, and the river is dark, peaceful, with a steamboat, dockbound after its dinner cruise, the only moving thing.

New Orleans, tourist trap or not, is a charmer.

However New Orleans is perceived, the city assaults the senses. There is, for example, the Superdome, now dominating downtown, which appears from a distance to be a giant Big Mac with pedestrian ramps. The Superdome began as a small multi-million dollar project and escalated into a megabucks monster costing almost $200 million. But it is at least a superb sports arena, and unique, if only because its artificial turf has the punned name of Mardi Grass—Instant Astrodome Trivia: At its normal eight knot per hour flow, how

long would it take the Mississippi River to fill the Superdome? Two and a half minutes. There are guided tours.

And food. Everyone speaks of New Orleans food.

Breakfast at Brennans. Oysters Rockefeller at Antoine's.
Mile High Ice Cream Pie at the Caribbean Room of Pont-
chartrain Hotel. The jazz brunch at Commander's Palace.
Creole Gumbo at my favorite unpronounceable restaurant,
Tchoupitoulas Plantation. Po-Boy Sandwiches anywhere.

A friend swears the best red beans and rice are served,
not in any formal New Orleans restaurant, but from neighborhood kitchens by housewives picking up a little extra
money. Neighbors know where to go and buy, but few others
do. Ask around.

New Orleanians eat in style, at all times, in all places.
I breakfasted one recent morning at a Canal Street drug store
counter, dining on a three-egg omelette, two large sausages, a
bowl of grits and three homemade fluffy bisquits as large as
pot lids. A buck eighty-nine plus tax. Another day it was the
Camellia Grill, a 14-stool establishment, for a chili omelette
and pecan pie. $2.75.

I arrived at the Camellia Grill via New Orleans' last
streetcar line. The St. Charles Avenue trollies depart every
few minutes from Canal Street, move through the Garden
District, the River Bend section, into the Carrollton area,
then return on the same route. A pleasant, nostalgic ride.

Coffee and beignets at the French Market's Cafe du
Monde is another tradition for a midnight snack. Beignets
are powdered sugary doughnuts without holes. Three to an
order. The coffee is strong and chicory flavored. Eighty-five
cents. I remember the price because the waiter never returned
with my change, which is another fine old New Orleans
tradition.

Always a genuine pleasure to visit New Orleans and its
Royal Street elegance, its voodoo dolls and sugary doughnuts,
nuder-than-nude dancers and decadent waiters who steal
your change. America's finest tourist trap. Wear your plantation-white suit and carry your wallet in your mouth. Good
luck.

UNCLE ARY AND HIS SLANTED PIGS...

1975

A SLANTED PIG CHRISTMAS

She was small and vital, my grandmother, a thin sheaf of nervous energy encased in a checkered apron and poke bonnet, and he, my grandfather, was a tall, quiet man with a face weathered and rough as barn wood. She made biscuits from scratch and deep-fried sugar pies and hand-stitched flour sack underwear for me. He could plow straight furrows behind mules and a neighbor once praised him lavishly, "Hilman shore keeps his cotton weeded good."

We lived during the war years in a farmhouse amid two hundred acres invested with cotton and corn. There was a chinaberry tree in the yard and old tires in which my grandmother grew flowers. The front porch was shady with wisteria vines and crowded with rocking chairs. There was neither electricity nor plumbing. We used coal oil lamps and wood stoves and, forty paces out back, a two-holer. A small barn, two sheds, a pesky herd of chickens, three cows, two mules and a cellar, to which my grandmother insisted we go at the first suspicion of rain, surrounded the small house. Across the dirt lane in front was a garden and an orchard with peach trees and blackberry vines and nearby a creek branch flowed through a thicket of scrub oaks. The Nolans lived down there apiece, and Buck and J. C. had an old house up the road. The Birches lived a mile west. Uncle Ary's farm adjoined our land on the north. Altogether, it was a bucolic life in North Central Texas while Hitler tried to conquer the world.

It was there in '43 that we ate Uncle Ary's Slanted Pig for Christmas dinner.

Uncle Ary was a round little old man always dressed in khaki pants and shirts and a snap-brimmed dress straw hat, even when plowing with his Ford tractor. His face was pinched with wrinkles and he rarely smiled. He was a life-long bachelor, and people said he was queer-acting. Perhaps he was. Uncle Ary *did* shout "Whoa!" when he wanted his Ford tractor to stop. He lived on his farm with peacocks and pigeons, wild ducks, a parrot and Miz' Lawson, his long-widowed first cousin and only living relative. She stayed in a cabin near the main house, cooked and washed for Uncle Ary.

Right up until his time to go, Uncle Ary believed the U.S. Government—especially President Roosevelt—was hiding his pig medal. It was his. He had worked for it, done his duty for America, and he wanted it. The government owed him and he always said FDR had told his federal men to hide the medal. He guessed it was somewhere in the White House, perhaps in the attic or the garage, both of which were good places to hide things.

Uncle Ary did his best to shake his pig medal out of Washington. He wrote letters, dozens of letters, to congressmen and senators and bureaucrats in the agricultural department, and once even to J. Edgar Hoover asking—politely, for Uncle Ary believed J. Edgar Hoover was our greatest living American—that the FBI arrest President Roosevelt and rescue the pig medal. Except for Sam Rayburn, nobody in Washington ever answered (J. Edgar probably was out on a Nazi spy ring job, Uncle Ary reasoned). Mr. Sam, the House Speaker, sent Uncle Ary a nice note saying the war effort was a success ". . . because of concerned citizens as yourself." Mr. Sam included a Department of Agriculture pamphlet on modern swine breeding methods.

Uncle Ary knew how to breed pigs and the pamphlet made him so mad he threw rocks at Homer Hanlon. Homer daily ran the Rural Free Delivery mail route in his 1936 Ford sedan. He was the only government man Uncle Ary knew, and so he believed Homer was immediately responsible for Washington's silence on the pig medal matter. Uncle Ary hid in tall Johnson grass beside his mail box and hit Homer's car twice with rocks as it sped by. That made Homer so mad he refused to deliver mail at all and for the rest of his life Uncle Ary had to drive to Hico for his letters, which never included medals from the government.

The postmaster came to Uncle Ary's farm to explain that having Rural Free Delivery did not automatically give somebody the right to throw rocks at mailmen just because they did not like the letters they received.

"You a Jew?" Uncle Ary asked of the postmaster.

The man, as Uncle Ary, was a lifelong, born-again, creek-dipped, tabernacle-trained, tithing Southern Baptist. He threatened to whip Uncle Ary for calling him a Jew. Uncle Ary picked up several average-sized throwing rocks. Miz' Lawson arrived about that time and the men had to stop cussing each other. The postmaster left mad, and Uncle Ary and Miz' Lawson wandered to the house for supper. Uncle Ary beat off the pigs with a big stick. He hated all pigs, but especially his pigs.

After supper, they sat on the porch and looked out on the peacocks and pigeons and pigs, and Uncle Ary said angrily, "That man was a Jew." Miz' Lawson tsk-tsked and patted Uncle Ary's arm consolingly.

"One of Roosevelt's Jews," he continued. "I can tell 'em a mile and a half away."

Miz' Lawson, who had never seen a Jew in her life or knew anyone who had, nodded.

Uncle Ary sighed, and said, "I'm almost sorry I invented them slanted pigs."

As a point of fact, Uncle Ary did not actually *invent* slanted pigs, but he did produce the first matched set, and later became the world's leading producer with an even dozen. It could be said Uncle Ary *developed* slanted pigs. That would be a fair statement. Where he got the original model, no one knew. He drove to Hico for his supplies one week and returned with the slanted pig. It was an ugly little beast with stunted front legs and small head and a hump along the back. At the rear the legs and flanks were enormous. The grotesque arrangement—an approximate recreation could be devised by mounting Mack Truck tires on the rear of a Volkswagen— made it appear as if the pig perpetually walked downhill.

Word got around and neighbors gossiped about the strange pig. "You hear 'bout that hunchbacked pig Ary got?" Mr. Nolan asked my grandfather. They went to see the pig.

Uncle Ary's slanted pig became an attraction and object

of derision. Loafers around the general store in Clairette guffawed and called "Oink, Oink" after Uncle Ary whenever he appeared there to replenish his supply of Bull Durham smoking tobacco. Uncle Ary ignored them. He knew his slanted pig was special.

Along in the spring of 1940 Uncle Ary purchased a regular pig, a smallish, sorrowful-faced sow. He put the sow with the slanted pig and allowed them free rein on their sexual urges. The sow may have believed she was being attacked by Quasimodo. Soon there were two more slanted pigs, perfect carbon copies of the original. The deformities, it seems, were genetic, and Uncle Ary was on his way to owning a full drove of slanted pigs, all runty, all with stunted front legs, hunched backs, disproportionately large flanks and rear trotters. They were a sight.

Soon after Pearl Harbor, Uncle Ary read in *Progressive Farmer* of the government's program to develop a "Battleship Hog," a swine breed larger and meatier than ever before, and of the Iowa farmer whose pigs were cited for their immensity. The Agricultural Department gave the farmer a medal. Uncle Ary devoted considerable thought to that. He reread the article, looked upon his burgeoning flock of leaning pigs with their oversized rear ham hocks and decided to do something for his country.

"The government's gonna give me a pig medal," he told Miz' Lawson. She nodded.

Thus Uncle Ary began his letter-writing campaign to Washington. Silence. More letters. More silence. Anger. Uncle Ary wanted his pig medal. The tilted pigs were gregarious little creatures, and horny, and by the fall of '43, they had begat and begat and become a flock of twelve monstrous little sloped creatures roaming freely through the peacocks and pigeons. Uncle Ary hated them.

By then, too, he was convinced Roosevelt's Jews were hiding his pig medal. Everybody knew Jews didn't eat pigs, he told Miz' Lawson, and the Jews didn't want Americans to have those oversized hams. That's why Washington didn't forward his pig medal. Miz' Lawson tut-tutted sympathetically.

In early December, we chopped down a cedar tree and mounted it in the parlor, strung it with popcorn and paper chains and little stars covered by tinfoil. Christmas was near.

Each winter, Miz' Lawson spent a week with her late husband's youngest sister, who lived near Round Rock, and one crisp morning she and Uncle Ary drove away in his old Chevy coupe. Later, Miz' Lawson told of the tragedy.

South of Temple, the coupe developed a flat left rear tire, and Uncle Ary pulled to the side, dismounted. He hunkered down to repair the tire. As luck would have it, he was struck by the third truck of an Army convoy from Fort Hood. There beside the road, Uncle Ary died.

The soldiers were distressed by the fatal accident and the wailing Miz' Lawson, but none more than the convoy commander, a Captain Goldstein, plucked by the military from his native Chicago to train on the dusty pastures of Fort Hood. As related by Miz' Lawson, the captain knelt over Uncle Ary to comfort the old man. Uncle Ary briefly opened his eyes, read the captain's nametag. Uncle Ary shouted at Goldstein, "Where you hidin' my pig medal!" and passed on.

A detail of soldiers drove Uncle Ary's Chevy and Miz' Lawson home, following the hearse. My grandmother and other community women brought covered dishes and the men cared for the livestock, even the pesky slanted pigs. After the funeral, Miz' Lawson gave the pigs away. Buck and J. C. took two, butchered and hung the meat in their smokehouse. The Nolans accepted another. The pigs were distributed to the neighbors. Only the Birches refused. They, being Campbellites, cited Biblical passages and declared the slanted pigs were children of the Devil.

We took one of the young piglets. My grandfather killed it and sliced off the hams, which fed all the relatives Christmas day. Afterwards the men gathered in the rocking chairs on the shady front porch and talked of Uncle Ary and his peculiar pigs. All of the little creatures must have been butchered and eaten because I've never again seen a slanted pig.

1980
PASSING

She was one of those Land's Sake and Mercy Me women, a beatitude in an old print dress, and he was tall and quiet and solemn with the inner peace of a Buddhist monk, though the analogy would offend his Baptist soul. He died first, in his eighties and very tired, and she wept softly and privately, then washed and folded his clothes, packed his worn farm tools in cardboard boxes, and gave everything to others. She kept nothing of her husband but a few faded photos and 55 years of memories.

When she died a decade later, also in her eighties and tired, her passing was as calm and untraumatic as his. Neither feared death because neither had feared life. After her funeral the family gathered and someone remarked that an era had died with the old man and woman, that a chapter of traditional ideas and ideals, customs and social mores had closed on American Southern life that could never be reopened. Not really, of course. Not yet. Eras don't end with the deaths of individuals but are dissolved by time until the generational images are too dim to register on the collective human psyche. The past becomes textbook footnotes and museum displays.

But too soon, within the framework of history, the era of the old man and woman will die and its passing, I think, is to be as dramatic as the disappearance of dinosaurs. Their generation is the last to have been born in and nourished by rural America. Forever after the world is urban, scientific, glossy, and perhaps unredeemably complex.

The old couple was born into a society little changed in four or five centuries. It was agrarian and simple, though often hard and harsh, that final decade of the nineteenth century, a time when Southern America's philosophy was a trinity of land, God, and work. Each came into life in a rough chinked-log farmhouse hardly different from those first built by our Pilgrims almost three hundred years earlier. Their food came from the land. Clothes mostly were sewn at home. Transportation was wagon, buggy, and horse. Their religion was taken in the community-built church of hand-sawed planks, a homely structure heated by wood stove, lighted by lamps, possessed only of crude benches and a poorly made lectern for the part-time preacher who took his pay in chickens and roasting ears.

They met and married in the early twentieth century, found 150 acres in Central Texas, rented a mule, and began farming, unaware that in the life beyond theirs, the phenomenon historians would call The Industrial Revolution was forever redesigning the future. They began a family as countries of the world indulged in a global war somewhere beyond their small farm. The first child died. The second and third survived. The fourth died. In the year Lindbergh flew the Atlantic, the cotton crop was excellent and they celebrated by ordering a suit for him, a church dress for her, new shoes for the children from the Sears & Roebuck catalog—and fretted for years about the extravagance.

When the depression arrived, neither they nor any of their neighbors were affected by it, as though they were stones in a river unmoved by the swiftly running current of history and change. In 1939 he bought the first family car. He was 44. She was afraid of it.

In the 1940's their small farmhome still was heated by wood stoves. Rural electrification had not arrived, nor had indoor plumbing and telephones. The farm was a calm place with an orchard, cows for milk and butter, chickens for eggs. He rose before dawn each day, stoked the fire, read his Bible by lamplight, and went to the fields. She cooked and canned and planted flowers around the porch, milked and churned and washed clothes in a black pot under the chinaberry tree. They helped their neighbors as the neighbors helped them.

The daughter married a town man and left. The son was drafted into another global war beyond the farm. He went away and never came back, and for the rest of the couple's lives they were distressed because his body could not be returned home for burial.

Finally, in the late 1950s the farm was sold and they moved to town, into another small frame house. He brought his farm tools with him, kept them oiled and polished should they ever have to return.

Except that they now lived in town, their lives changed little. They still arose before dawn, read the Bible, helped their neighbors. She still made biscuits from scratch and exquisite fruit pies. There was a garden out back for the vegetables she canned. He bought a radio, though never a television. Each found part-time jobs because idleness offended their Puritan souls. Together they chose their gravesites and planned their funerals, neither of which would come for more than 20 years.

There was a benign innocence about them. Man walked on the moon and they walked, holding hands, to the neighborhood church. Communications were instantaneous and worldwide, and they chose to talk with neighbors on the front porch at sunset. Great corporations spun out shiny gadgets holding all of mankind's knowledge since the beginning of time, built machines that flew in space, and he sat each evening in a rocker his father had bought in 1902. Grandchildren went off to summer in Europe and returned to grandparents who had never traveled more than 100 miles from where they were born. The old farm was absorbed into a larger agricultural complex worked by an incorporated man whose sons went to college to learn that the orchard planted in the year Henry Ford first produced Model T's was not cost efficient and thus had to be replaced by a money crop, while daily he had to work in the small town garden, had to feel the moist earth to recharge his spirit.

They were untouched and undisturbed by this Futureworld around them. He said he was proud that he once had walked eight miles to repay a $20 loan and that in all of his life he had never broken his word to any man. She believed food bought in store cans tasted of tin.

And so they died, he first, she later, and they were buried in the graves they had selected so many years earlier. They were gone and there was nothing to pass on, except memories and ancient photos, the old rocker and the pink brooch he had given her when they married. The era had not died with them, but little of it remained. There is less of it now and it will be smaller still tomorrow and the day after, until that quiescent age is gone forever, buried like the old couple in a grave.

1977

FAVORITE TEXAS WORDS

Texas expressions have a perfect feel of place but only if you have experienced the social and cultural and environmental processes which caused them. They are endemic of Texas, but anyone recently arrived from, say, Shaker Heights, Ohio, may believe he has stumbled across a study in Urdu.

It is, for instance, impossible to explain "peckerwood" to a Pennsylvanian who has never been called one.

"Peckerwood" was a term of endearment usually applied to a small boy by an older man. By some etymological magic, "peckerwood" was transposed from "woodpecker" (much as "sideburns" was subverted from the Civil War's General Burnsides, who wore muttonchop whiskers). See? The rational reaction by outsiders to "peckerwood" is "?" and rightly so.

Once I knew a lady from my early days. She was several years beyond 90, a Garrett Scotch Snuff dipper who nervously swabbed the stuff around her gums with the frazzled tip of an elm stick. She spoke hesitantly of her late husband's prize "he-cow." Being a properly brought-up West Texas lady she would never have said "bull" in mixed company. Her face reddened even with "he-cow" and had she not grown out of the habit no doubt she would have feigned a small Victorian swoon to fully register her embarrassment.

She spoke of many things, among them her conversion as a "shinnery-broke Baptist." "Shinnery" was the word for a brushy thicket of trees. She had come to Baptist conversion during a Sunday religious gathering at which people sat on "Baptist pallets" (quilts spread on the ground). The lady had been properly dipped into muddy waters of the Leon River by a "jakeleg preacher" (often written as "jackleg," it refers in this instance to someone "called" by the Lord; he "took up" preaching without benefit of formal training).

He, she explained, was a real man of God, not—this was spoken in a voice underlaid with elegant disgust for such devils —"one of them 'mama-called-daddy-sent' preachers." Such a minister was one whose mother said, "I want you to be a preacher." The boy's father sent him to seminary, where, the little lady believed, he was infused with "modernist" philosophies which, of course, were a plague on The True Word.

A catalogue of one-time semi-dirty cuss words: dad gum, durn, doggone, shucks, consarn, dad blame, dad burn it, dad rat it and gol dern.

For reasons I never understood, either a frog or a toad was commonly called a "toadfrog." Either one, or both. A "clucker" was a setting hen, that is, a hen sitting on eggs waiting for them to hatch.

Small boys never "threw" rocks in West Texas; they "chunked" rocks. Therefore a "chunking rock" was one with proper size and heft for "chunking." A "cob floater" was a heavy rain (a.k.a. "gully-washer," "frog strangler," and "trash mover").

No one *hunkers* anymore. A long time ago, everyone did. Hunkering was a favored West Texas pastime, for doing business, for just talking ("jawin"), for whittling on a mesquite stick. I have seen a dozen old men hunkered in a circle before a general store or a filling station, passing the day pleasantly. Cowhands hunkered together around the cow lots, doing a little trading.

You never see people hunkered at the supermarket or on their backyard patios. It is a lost art, and deserving of revival.

Try it the next time you're in Safeway.

THE ANCIENT ART
OF
HUNKERING

1968

EAST TEXAS

East Texas is . . . uh, oh, there's them trees, and . . . uh, it's kinda . . . uh, well, hell, son, I'll tell you, East Texas ain't no more'n West Texas, 'cept they got shade and we don't"—A West Texas Rancher attempting to describe East Texas, which he had never seen.

To understand East Texas you must know West Texas. An old cowboy, now long dead, once told me about East Texas. He lived south of Amarillo, in the Texas Panhandle, so he was prejudiced, but what he said was, "The only thing wrong with East Texas is that it's too durn confining. I like to see where I'm going day after tomorrow."

He lived in the Texas of official record, that mythical country with its straight-line horizon and flat, vacant space. West Texas has charisma. It has made Hollywood rich. Flat-bellied and lean-hipped John Waynes and Gary Coopers dwell there in boots and starched jeans, hats pulled low over dark, menacing eyes. Astride huge, white stallions they race across the vastness like summer lightning. In West Texas bloom red and black and white cattle, wisps of smeared color on the gray landscape of a late afternoon.

Outlanders know that Texas by heart—the boots and jeans sterotype, smells of old leather and cattle, Cadillacs and Neiman-Marcus suits for the Saturday night dance at the country club.

East Texas is something else. To begin with it is overalls, scents of dogwood and pine and fresh, green grass, Chevrolets and a blue serge from J.C. Penney's for the Saturday night dance at the American Legion hall.

East Texas has no vastness, no endlessness. Its forests

cause that, shutting you into cool, shady places, almost silent vacuums of flowers, pines and ponds. So you see East Texas in bits and pieces, like assembling a jigsaw puzzle. In West Texas you hear dry and twangy voices. The speech of East Texas favors hound dogs and quiet fishing holes, small farms and oil wells. A West Texan does not mind driving 100 miles for a beer. An East Texan drinks his bourbon and branch on the front porch.

In West Texas *the* tree is mesquite, an iron-skinned, thorny and generally warped-trunk thing favored by shade-starved cattle as a partial answer to the hot sun. East Texas has four national forests binding 658,000 acres of pine, magnolia, oak, cypress, wild plum, black haw, bay and sweet gum. There are thousands of privately owned forested acres, hiding sandy roads, natural pools of spring water, wild flowers and peacefulness.

East Texas, I guess, is trees and people, a different breed of Texan. The two Texans share only fierce independence and a common distaste for convention.

Some day Hollywood should attempt to capture on film a true scene of East Texas life, such as the elderly lady standing beside her front gate. The local sheriff drove up.

"Miz' Ferguson, I want to ask you some questions."

"Sheriff," she answered, "this is my land and here I'll ask the questions." And she did.

You can't overemphasize the trees. If you must put a boundary to East Texas, think trees. West, north or south, when the trees stop, East Texas stops. Purists claim East Texas stretches from Paris to Moscow, which is true. Paris is a town on the Oklahoma border. Moscow is a lumber village north of Houston.

Between these guide marks is East Texas and I tell you, here and now, that it is a special place.

"West Texas is a harsh, rude country and it took harsh, rude men to settle there. East Texas is softer, more gentle, and gentlemen were needed to live with it."—University professor's assessment of the two Texases.

In the 1600s the Spanish came as they always did, curious and conquering, claiming the land for kings who never would see it. Because God rode with them they founded missions along a trail which crossed Texas at what now is Toledo Bend Reservoir, Sabine and Davy Crockett national forests, the towns of San Augustine, Nacogdoches, Alto and Crockett, to San Antonio and, ultimately, to Mexico. They called it El Camino Real. A century later LaSalle decided the road was as much traveled as that "from Paris to Orleans."

Settlers moved into East Texas from Arkansas and Louisiana and other Southern states. Some say the farmers remained and the malcontents, the unsociable men with dark, hard eyes and searching souls, traveled west to do battle with that unfortunate country. If West Texans will admit the truth, East Texas gave them nearly everything they honor, except dust storms.

East Texans—the early ones—tended to cluster, causing hundreds of tiny settlements. Even today there are no large cities as we think of them. Tyler is largest with less than 100,000 population. Longview and Lufkin, Huntsville, Jacksonville, Palestine and Marshall are not large towns. Mostly the region has maintained a kind of suspended timepiece on that token of Americana that is too-quickly disappearing—the small town.

East Texans were inventive for their communities. There are common names, to be sure, but there are too Hoot Index, Swamppoodle Creek, Frognot, Honest, Old Granny's Neck, Bug Tussle, Fink, Mutt and Jeff, Cut 'n Shoot and the lyrical Sherry Prairie Cemetery. Most are only crossroads on the way to some place, but to find settlements like these you have to drive the backroads and the sandy logging trails.

Off the highways are the cabins whose owners oft-times live by trapping and fishing. In spring, and I think spring is best, the streams fill with rainwater and flowers color the ground: bluebonnets, Indian paintbrush, crimson clover, azaleas.

The Big Thicket, north of Houston and covering much of five counties, is an ecological marvel, sheltering in dark, almost ethereal splendor a curious gathering of plants and animals. More than 20 varieties of orchids grow wild. Here are giant ferns and palmettos, honeysuckle, sweet broom, and the meateaters—the bladderwort and the sundew—majestic cypress with Spanish-moss hanging specter-like over marshes. It is the home of alligator, otter, wild turkey and hogs and, even, the ivory-billed woodpecker, long believed to be extinct before being discovered again in the Big Thicket. This is the legacy of East Texas, a jungle of wonder.

I wish you had known Lance Rosier. He died recently, a skinny-necked, slump-shouldered, bright-eyed rare old man who never weighed more than 120 pounds in his life. With little formal education, Lance nevertheless was the world authority on plant life in the Big Thicket. Botanists—"those school doctors," he called them—came from as far away as South America, Japan and France to be taught by this old man of the forest.

Lance would walk his famous scientists into the Thicket and teach them its ways, correctly calling sweet broom *scopera adulcis* and the magnolia, *glauca, acuminata* or *florida*. Without Lance to guide you there are two spots to view in the Big Thicket. The first is a scenic area in Sam Houston National Forest, near Shepherd. There are marked trails. The second is the Alabama-Coushatta Indian Reservation near Livingston where a guide will show you the exotic landscape.

Lately Texans have become concerned about the shrinking Big Thicket and are priming Congress for assurance it will be saved as a national park or wilderness area.

Lance Rosier would have liked that.

"I got lost once in East Texas, down by Votaw, and I never enjoyed anything more"—A big city newspaperman's remembrance of East Texas.

Man has done well in East Texas. Author Mary Lasswell considered it a land of "caviar and clabber." Houston columnist Leon Hale claims East Texas is a place where men still dig their own fishing worms. In that statement is a profound moral too abstract for me, but I understand the superficial meaning. East Texas is a good place to sit a spell.

The place surprises you. Remember Moscow? Well, seven miles away is Camden, another logging town. A logging train still operates between Moscow and Camden, moving out of a huge sawmill to a railhead. You can ride along. Anyone can.

Oil is so prominent in East Texas some people are embarrassed about it. When Spindletop blew in at Beaumont on the East Texas Gulf Coast, the world changed, and the East Texas pool splashed a lot of wealth on the piney woods.

I remember a Central Texas cotton farmer's pained expression as he recalled his misfortune. "I left Longview in the mid-20s because I was tired of it. I had a hired hand on the place and he was a poor man with a lotta children. I gave him five acres. Wasn't worth $10 an acre. Wouldn't you know it, that five acres was sitting in the middle of that oil. And I gave it away. My hand got rich and him and all them kids drove over here one day in a big car . . . to thank me for giving him that land. I guess he did! He blame well better."

In East Texas' four national forests, four state forests, a dozen state parks and nearly two-dozen sizable lakes are more than 30 recreational areas with campgrounds, cabins, hiking trails, boat-launching facilities and picnic areas. All are connected to an excellent highway system.

The roads lead you to curious places, such as Jefferson, one of those timeless towns, once a steamboat termination point until the river changed its course. All of Jefferson is a museum piece. Today's Excelsior House Hotel contains antique furniture, some of which is over 100 years old. U. S. Grant, Oscar Wilde and Jay Gould slept there, although, as often as not, Gould stayed on his private railway car, which sits today outside the hotel.

Nearby is Caddo Lake, another of those eerie Texas spots, filled with moss-laden trees and narrow channels, floating islands and, I am told, whale-size bass. A unique side of Caddo is the 43-mile boat trail that lets you drift among the Gothic scenery without becoming lost, as many fishermen have.

You can't discuss East Texas without mentioning Karnack, which has been properly marked as the birthplace of

WEST TEXAN

EAST TEXAN

Lady Bird Johnson; Marshall, which was capital of Missouri during the Civil War; Woodville, with its Heritage Village preserving intact much of the history of the region; Huntsville, where each October convicts turn cowboy for the best rodeo in Texas; or Lake of the Pines; Sam Rayburn Lake; Mission Tejas; the new tourist train at Jacksonville; and Sulphur Springs, which has the best-preserved example of early courthouses.

All of this is East Texas, not an uncomfortable place at all. Sam Houston liked it and Davy Crockett almost remained in the forests rather than ride on to the Alamo. There are other, lesser-known East Texans, like Leon Hale's friend who, come spring, always thaws out his pet alligator underneath the kitchen stove. And the 93-year-old lady from Woodville who roams the state in Greyhound buses, preaching for conservation. These are nice people.

I asked a friend of mine in Tyler to explain East Texas for me. He lives Walden-style beside a forest lake, in a cabin he built himself.

He considered the question a long time before answering. "East Texas," he said slowly, "is just East Texas, that's all." And so it is.

1972

BAH! ON BASEBALL

With a stifled yawn and a weary id I plan to avoid watching the World Series this week. Maybe they will go away quickly and we can get on with the business of football.

I am perfectly aware there are millions of baseball fans out there aching for The Great American Pastime to fill their empty hours. But there are those of us who will not welcome the intrusion of A's and Reds into our living room.

This week we non-baseball fans either watch "Gilligan's Island" re-runs or do these long-neglected odd jobs to pass the time until baseball is gone for another year.

Baseball, I think, is not a sport for television. For two-and-a-half hours you get shots of nine guys leaning on their kneecaps and two voices saying what a great game baseball is.

There are long interminable pictures of the pitcher shaking his head at the catcher and first base coaches scuffing cleated toes in the ground and a guy dressed in black whisk-brooming dust off a rubber plate called home base.

When there finally is some action it is so brief that an eyeblink will cause you to miss it.

A baseball fan tells me I should view baseball like a chess game, that it chiefly is a game of strategy and subtle maneuvers. But I am too impatient to follow a game this way.

I want something to happen. And it doesn't in baseball. Football has ruined televised baseball. Football is a sport in which action falls over action. Football is active; baseball is passive.

Baseball did not seem an uninteresting sport when I was younger, nor does it cause a feeling of boredom when you see a game in person.

But television has exposed it as a slow, deadly dull game.

Maybe baseball would be better if it were left alone without television.

Good ole Abner Doubleday would not like the way his game of baseball has been televised to tedium.

Abner, on second thought, probably would not care at all, since it is likely he had nothing to do with the game. I took an extensive survey among four people the other day and three of them still credited Abner Doubleday with being the originator of baseball.

He is not. And that bit of fiction was exposed years ago.

One of the baseball books of my youth stated that Abner, a West Point cadet, invented the game at Cooperstown, N.Y., in 1839.

It is unlikely Doubleday was even in Cooperstown (where the Baseball Hall of Fame was established to celebrate the legend) that year.

Doubleday, who became a general and hero at the battle of Gettysburg, never claimed he originated baseball. Others did, but only after his death in 1893.

We got baseball from an English game called "Rounders." And "Rounders" was played in America as early as 1778. And perhaps even 30 years before that.

There is evidence that soldiers at Valley Forge took a little time off from freezing and starving to play "Rounders," which they called "base."

Princeton had a "baste ball" game as early as 1786.

So Abner didn't do it.

A fireman in New York, Alexander Cartwright, is credited with forming the first basic rules for American baseball—in 1845.

The reason Abner Doubleday was for so long known as the father of baseball was that early baseball moguls wanted him to have the honor.

Early baseball was anything but totally honest. There were gambling scandals and player stealing and general dishonesty (like players throwing games).

Baseball yearned for respectability. A public relations program tried to sell the game as purely American and good clean fun. Few believed either claim.

So in 1903 a commission appointed by several baseball club owners set out to prove the game was as American as anything.

Three years later the commission issued its findings. Abner Doubleday, it said, invented baseball in 1839 at Cooperstown.

Everybody was happy.

In 1939 baseball decided to hold a centennial and commemorate Doubleday's remarkable game.

Many people still believe the fiction today. Not that it is important, except to sports historians who know "Rounders" was the pre-baseball game and it was English, not American.

A principal difference between "Rounders" and baseball is that in the former you could throw the ball at a runner. If you hit him he was out.

This was called "dousing" or "soaking."

That sounds like a good addition to the new game of baseball.

And it might get my attention again.

Eighteen guys throwing baseballs at one another is far better than "Gilligan's Island."

1971
WHEN A PUN'S SPUN

Puns are crimes. Justified homicide, in all cases. I like them. A man who puns will commit many gross sins against nature. He is not a guy to hang around with. He is worth avoiding because he is sure to tell you about the old Apache who registered his boys in a local yacht club.

Seems he wanted to see his red sons in the sail set.

Or the tale of Mr. Fligh, whose lifetime occupation was setting hands in a clock factory. He was good at his job.

"My, my," said a co-worker one day, "how Fligh times."

Or the sad account of two boy silkworms who chased after a pretty girl silkworm. They ended up in a tie.

Shorties: "What's a crick? (the noise made by a Japanese camera) and what's a small dog suffering from chills? (a pupsickle).

Nothing on earth is as damnable as a pun. It unnerves people. It causes common sense people to reach for ax handles

I'VE NEVER SAUSAGE A THING LIKE THIS BEFORE!
AR·AR·AR···

with which to beat the offender. The man who told this should be publicly whipped:

Once when invaders overcame Czechoslovakia, a patriot sought refuge in an American embassy. "Surely," he asked, "you won't mind caching a small Czech?"

The next time you want to drive your friends nuts, tell them about the guy in Tibet. One day his barn caught fire. He smelled something burning. "Oh," he cried, "my baking yak."

Paranomasia is the word for pun. It means the tendency to tell atrocious puns. It is a disease, I think. You will notice it sounds much like paranoid.

So punsters are sick. Historians claim Adam made the first pun. "What's wrong with eating this ole apple?" asked Eve. "I'll bite," answered Adam. And the next day God threw them out of the garden. I don't blame Him.

As civilization went downhill, puns grew more elaborate. In 846 A.D., a shepherd sent his son out one night to tend the sheep. The boy took an oil lamp with him. He became sleepy and lay down under a tree. He slept. His lamp burned out. His father found him and was angry. The father told the son his punishment would be to tend the sheep for the next seven nights. Without a lamp.

"Oh," said the son, "do give me a new wick for my lamp."

"No, sleepyhead," replied the father, "there is no wick for the rested."

Later, along about 1700, two men sat down at a sidewalk cafe in Paris. One ordered wine. The other asked for a cup of water. Shortly the waiter returned and asked if they wanted something else.

"Bring him another glass of wine," said one, "and I'll have a little more of the Seine."

As society became more corrupt, puns gained in power. In America, along the Mississippi River, there was a showboat captain and his wife who had 16 children, all of whom were in the various plays presented on the boat. Supposedly they were the first couple who bred their cast upon the waters. Punning even spread to the inscrutable Chinese. A certain Charlie Chan, the detective. Mr. Chan was the repeated victim of a thief. The midnight visitor was stealing small miniatures made of teakwood. The detective found footprints of a small boy.

Late one evening Mr. Chan hid in his living room, waiting for the thief. Turned out to be a huge black bear with—as coincidence would have it—the feet of a little boy.

Naturally the private eye had to say, "Heh, there! Where do you think you're going, oh boy-foot bear with teaks of Chan?"

Even cities got into the punning business. Places like Metro, Cal., Oola, La., Hittor, Miss., Praise, Ala., Fiven, Tenn., and Goodness, Me.

Absolutely the worst pun to which I have been subjected lately concerns a guy who owned four porpoises. He kept them in a backyard pool. One day a guru told him how to keep them alive forever: Feed the porpoises sea gulls.

So . . . the man went to the seashore and captured a bagful of gulls. When he returned home he found a lion lying in front of his door. The lion was asleep. Gently, the guy lifted his bag of gulls and stepped over the lion.

Naturally police had to arrest him—for transporting gulls across a prostrate lion for immortal porpoises.

Now that's a bad pun.

LORD BYRON NELSON

1979

FOR LORD BYRON NELSON, STILL THE MUSIC LINGERS

It is one of those days made of yellow daisies and sun-shine, a time of purest spring when lovers sigh and breezes actually whiffle through fresh grasses like they do in verses composed by old ladies in Victorian mansions, and you are pleased some Scottish herdsman of antiquity seized on that gnarled stick and began striking a round rock to ease his boredom.

You are out there 260 yards in the middle of No. 18, and half of Dallas is massed behind the fairway ropes while two teenagers anesthetized by the whiffling breezes kiss under an oak tree in defiance of TV cameras and propriety, and Lee Trevino stalks the alignment of a 25-foot putt up there on the green.

You ask for a 6-iron, milk the grip twice, and wait.

Back there you had it all to yourself, two strokes up and coasting. Then Trevino, one of the game's great hustlers, struck a 4 wood 270 yards, which is only humanly impossible, laid in a 15-foot eagle, and walked away winking at the ladies, chattering, all even and coming on. You heard the cheers and knew. You got out there, and on, and snaked in a birdie. Back up a stroke. At 17 Trevino busted a long iron, a short iron, and a 12-foot putt. Birdie. Even again. You hit a 4 wood, a wedge, then hesitated over a 20 footer. You stroked. It rolled up, around the cup's edge, backed in. Bird. One stroke lead, and going home.

And there on the 18th is Trevino, with his punch-putt style, stroking the ball to the hole and three inches beyond. Tap in. Par. One stroke short. He takes the cheers and turns to watch you back there 165 yards with your 6 iron. Your turn.

You set up, look, look again, and swing. Anxious, you come over the ball and it hooks away as the teenagers kiss and the crowd, as one, groans. The ball twists left of the green, behind the deep trap, under a tree, finally sitting on a slope of hard, bare graveled earth, and high in the TV tower the familiar voice says, "He is capable of making that shot. The shot can be made." None of those Sunday golfers in their living rooms believes the voice. It is an impossible shot. Simply impossible.

Moments later, you hold your wedge, standing uncomfortably on the slanted ground, and all around is a museum silence. You take a deep breath, let it out, and tell yourself to do it.

Your name, by the way, is Tom Watson.

• • •

They call him, with a kind of irreverent fondness, The Lord, and The Lord was late.

"Anybody seen The Lord?" Somebody asked in the press tent.

Heads shook. The inevitable wisecrack came: "The Lord moves in mysterious ways."

It was cool, cold for May in north Texas where hot is

common even in midspring. There were clouds the color of second-day bruises and a nipping wind and no pretty girls in shorts and halters, which is usual in north Texas when professional golf comes to town.

A big black man, Jim Dent of Georgia, stepped onto the first tee box at 8:16 a.m. and punched the ball toward Oklahoma, and perhaps got there. His gallery, a paunchy man and his bright-eyed son, walked away with Dent. On that dark day when the wind came from five directions at once and the mud was glutenous, the temperature 46 degrees, and with sportswriters already calling it The Great Igloo Open, only hard-core golfing fans were out for first shots of the Byron Nelson Golf Classic at Dallas' Preston Trail Golf Club.

Even The Lord was late. Lord Byron, as they knighted him back there in the Middle Ages of golf when guys played for bed and board and little more. John Byron Nelson, a legend. No, more than that. A golfing legend from Texas.

To understand why many good—great—golfers are made in Texas would require a psychological briefing on the macho-cum-hystericus makeup of the state. We do not enjoy losing; losing is, somehow, unmanly, and unthinkable. Just know that right now there are boys and girls having golf sticks thrust into their hands and being told to go out and compete. Recently, in a Fort Worth junior tournament, a six-year-old boy shot a 57 on nine holes. The kid is learning.

Maybe that's why last year Texas golfers took 12% of all pro golf purses. More than $1.1 million in a year when 289 pro golfers won money. Fewer than 1% of the pro golfers won 12% of the money. How else to explain it than being Texan?

Miller Barber, Trevino, Don January, Ben Crenshaw, Tom Kite—Texans all, and winners. There are others, but you get the idea.

It's the wind, some say, explaining how and why Texas golfers exert dominance on the pro golf tour. Even Byron Nelson says it.

He came after lunch, with the weather warmer and crowds larger, a blocky man with a quick stride. He has those red jowls and white hair and merry eyes characteristic of a grandfather and the snap-brim hat that has become a trademark. He moved through the people massed near the clubhouse and stepped behind ropes onto the practice range.

"There's no one reason why Texas produces so many golfers, but learning golf here, in the heat, the wind, the cold, you're schooled under different conditions," he said. "In this area we practice a lot against the wind, which exaggerates a fade or a hook or whatever you hit. If you learned to hit it well against the wind, you can sure play when there isn't much wind. And we play 12 months a year here. And for years we've had good junior golf programs in Texas. Even when Ben [Hogan] and I came along, if a boy wanted to play, it was never a problem finding a place to play and someone to let him play."

Nelson and Hogan were caddies at Fort Worth's Glen Garden Country Club, competing even then against one another. Each won the club's caddy championship. By 1930 Nelson became Southwest Amateur champion and in 1932 won $75 in his first pro tourney. He won The Masters in 1937, the first of two championships there, and the U.S. Open in 1939.

Lord Byron played in the post-knickers era after Jones and Hagen and before Palmer and Nicklaus, and no one, not Hogan, nor Sam Snead, played better. There is credible evidence that no one has ever played the game as well as Byron Nelson. "At my best," Bobby Jones once said, "I never came close to the golf Nelson shoots."

Nelson played at his best during World War II when golf was at its lowest. The British Open wasn't played in those years. The Vardon Trophy was not awarded for several years. The better golfers were off at war. So Byron Nelson's career has the taint of no real competition. Except golf is played against a fixed score, a course, yourself—and Nelson beat all, especially in 1945.

In 1945, Nelson entered 30 of 32 professional tournaments. All he did was win 18, including 11 in a row. He finished 2nd seven times and 3rd in another tourney; 4th,

5th, 6th, and 10th in four others. For 19 consecutive rounds he shot under 70 strokes, and for 120 rounds his stroke average was 68.33. At today's golf prices, Nelson would have collected half a million dollars. He won $52,511.32. And retired. He bought a 600-acre ranch north of Dallas/Fort Worth and became a rancher.

He never really left golf. He played a little, winning the 1955 French Open, and became a golf TV commentator. But Byron Nelson's value to the game today is that of teacher. He has become a kind of guru to young players, amateur and pro alike. They come to the mountain—meaning the Preston Trail Golf Club—for help from the old master. And why not? Byron Nelson invented today's swing style—the straight high takeaway, the weight shift, the knees/feet interaction. He knows every piece of it, so the youngsters come.

Johnny Miller and Tony Lema and Bobby Nichols. Nelson tutored Ken Venturi into the U.S. Open championship. And Tom Watson. Watson credits Nelson with his victories in The Masters and British Open and the $300,000 plus he collected as 1977's leading money winner. Watson has joined Preston Trail, as a nonresident member, to be near Byron Nelson.

That cool day when Lord Byron stepped onto the practice tee at his tournament—the only tournament named for a golfer—Ben Crenshaw moved quickly to his side. And Tom Weiskopf. The men began talking golf in a language understood only by engineers and anatomists. Ben would hit a ball; Nelson would watch and comment. Weiskopf showed his grip; Nelson nodded.

"Oh, we were just talking golf," Nelson commented later, as though the trio were plumbers discussing drain pipes.

No, he couldn't predict a winner of the tourney, though Watson had been playing well. And Lee Trevino.

That morning, Trevino fed his kids, made coffee for his wife, took out the garbage, and went to work. He is the perfect Texas golfer, outwardly gregarious and chatty, but burning inside to win. Trevino grew up in Dallas, far away from the dark-mahogany life-style of Preston Trail. And he was a hustler. He still will play you using only a Dr Pepper bottle and a cut ball, if you put your money up, but don't count on getting it back. He learned to play at Tenison, a municipal course, using taped-together clubs.

There was a special game for guts players at Tenison. Everybody put up $5 apiece, and they played from first tee to ninth green, 900 yards away, and did it in a forest of trees and through a narrow two-man tunnel under a railroad track. Trevino learned to hit the ball through the tunnel on the first crack, straight through like a clothesline, and fade it afterwards beyond a big oak. He still can do it.

Watson and Trevino played well that first day, but not spectacularly, as crowds shivered and slogged through mud up to their fetlocks. Dent, helped by a miraculous 100-foot putt, was the leader. He held the lead through Friday, and the sun came out.

With the sun came people, 40,000 of them, and girls in shorts and halters. Crowds followed Palmer, hoping for the old magic to return.

When the halcyon days of spring finally arrived, so had Watson. He took the lead Saturday. Two strokes back, Trevino said he still could win Sunday by shooting 66. Lord Nelson came early those two final warm days, climbing high into the ABC-TV tower over 18. Before airtime he spoke of the sport he had dominated one year as no man before or since.

"There are more good players now, although if you leave out Nicklaus the rest of the top players are no better than Snead, Hogan, Demaret, Middlecoff, and maybe me. But with so many, it's hard to finish 10th. We knew who we had to beat; now there are 30 or so players capable of winning. Courses now get more water and fertilizer. The fairways are softer; the greens are better. Nothing has progressed so much as golf agronomy. The size of galleries now forces them to rope the crowd off. Makes it easier because they used to be in the fairways, walk with you, talk with you. It's harder to concentrate that way. I've had people in the gallery trip me by accident."

What about the equipment? Some better, he allowed, but the swing was the thing. Today it's all swing. Repeating the repeatable swing. Nelson understands that, which is why the PGA's mechanical ball-testing club is called The Iron Byron. It re-creates the perfect swing every time, the way Byron Nelson learned to do it. Back there between 1932 and 1937, when he wasn't winning much, Nelson, like a shade-tree mechanic, had taken his game apart, spread the pieces on the grass, and studied each part with the mind of an analytical scientist.

In pieces, his game wasn't much. Hogan was a better driver—even Bob Hope once outdrove Nelson in an exhibition. Snead was a better iron player. Demaret could putt truer. Taken all together, though, his game was unbeatable, especially in 1944 and 1945, when it all finally came together and other players began learning from Nelson, copying what he had innovated.

On that final day, as Watson was coasting, and Trevino was reaching for his 4 wood, and the yellow daisies and sunshine burst into springtime, loafers around the clubhouse were telling old Texas golfing stories, of the course out near Lubbock where you had to carom shots off mesquite tree trunks in order to score well, and a sudden wind that blew a ball into the men's room, and that little course down near Waco that used to have sand greens and cows munching on the fairways and how you cut a slice by smearing Vaseline on your clubhead.

Byron Nelson was not a part of that. He never smoked nor drank nor hung out in clubhouses with the boys after a round nor, he once said, ever played a round of golf he was satisfied with. Perfection is a mean playing partner.

But he knows the game better than any man alive. Back there three or four years ago Tom Watson had those Huck Finn freckles and poise and a good swing. The next Nicklaus, everybody said. Except that Watson wasn't winning that much. In 1974, he was leading in the third round of the U.S. Open, then on the final day posted a 79. Afterwards, in the clubhouse, Nelson approached the dejected young Watson.

In a corner, the older man talked quietly. Of knees not

working through a shot, of coming out of the shot too soon, of lifting up, staying on the right side too long. Watson took Nelson's advice. Two weeks later he won the Western Open. After the 1975 U.S. Open, Nelson warned Watson to slow down the movement of his feet, and he thought about that as he later won the British Open. There was more advice and titles and money, and today if you want to see Byron Nelson on a golf course, look at Tom Watson.

• • •

And you think about all those little things as you stand there uncomfortable on the hard sloped ground, under the tree, behind the trap with Trevino finished and holding his predicted winning score of 66 and Nelson's smooth voice telling television viewers, "The shot can be made."

You tell yourself to do it, relax and swing and the ball clicks up, under the tree branches, over the trap, plops onto the soft green, skids 8 inches, and stops 2½ feet from the hole. The shot is possible, as Nelson reminds.

Moments later, you stroke it in to win again, becoming, almost incidentally, pro golf's 17th millionaire.

1983

EL PASO

The desert is a disease, and its own antidote. Out here, in this far flat corner of Texas, it is the only physical truth, a terrible-tempered tyrant raging with dust and heat, loneliness and unremitting linear distance.

Outsiders find a little desert goes a long way.

For those who have chosen to live here beyond nuclear Texas, the desert is a kind of benevolent malady whose very presence is the substance of their existence. For them the desert is soothing, calming, a beige treeless sea of tranquility surrounding the concrete island that has become El Paso.

They may be right.

The desert, I admit, has a rough, raw beauty almost magnetic in its grim immensity. It is a medicine of the psyche and I feel better for having taken a dose of desert, though I have determined more treatments at this time are not required.

El Pasoans would disagree with me. I am suspicious of them. They elected to settle in this austere region and appear to be perfectly content with their city and its desert. Why? What do they know that we don't? Why have they gathered way out here? Who are these people and what do they want?

Whatever else El Paso may be, it is unlike Texas. El Pasoans and Tyler rose farmers are Texans, may reside in the same state, but the similarity ends there. They could as well be Finnish Lapp reindeer ranchers and Greek shopkeepers— each is European but neither has anything in common with the other.

It concerns me that El Pasoans have no accent, no West Texas twang, no nasal verbal burr as the rest of us. The accent has disappeared, perhaps sandpapered away by the blowing dust or melded with the softness of border Spanish. For whatever reasons, it is gone, just as, for whatever reasons, West Texas vanishes somewhere out beyond Pecos where the high desert takes over.

This is not West Texas, but Western Texas, an unknown country, a kind of independent nation that exists for itself alone, so non-Texas that the Dallas Cowboys are given only tacit support and, from my experience, you can't find a decent chicken-fried steak. This, truly, is a hardship land.

With Tucson and Phoenix, El Paso is among America's most distant communities (when the world ends, El Paso won't know about it until a week later, a local historian once decided). No one just stumbles upon El Paso. You must want to come here, guided by the same inner compulsions that led Lewis and Clark into Oregon Territory or Moses into the Promised Land, must purposely set your aim at the gap in the Franklin Mountains through which Spanish conquistadores passed five centuries ago in search of golden cities.

Isolation is El Paso's cross, but also, possibly, its salvation, because it has been forced to create its own functioning civilization quite apart from the rest of us. El Paso transcends Texas. It and Juarez, across this cement ditch serving as the Rio Grande, have coupled to become a self-dependent bi-national city of a million people correctly unconcerned with wheat crop failures in the Panhandle or polluted beaches in Acapulco and political intrigue in Austin or Mexico City.

Do lobby-bought Austin politicians shrink from the Texas horse-betting question? Not to worry. The ponies are running at Sunland Park of New Mexico, a suburb of El Paso, and in Juarez. Peso devaluation from Mexico City? So what. Juarez deals in dollars, too. Blue laws? Never heard of them. El Paso/Juarez is autonomous.

To come upon El Paso of the '80s by air or by highway is to find an uncommonly far place of desert America, spread before the final gray crags of the Rockies, an accident of time and space. Settled amid the desert starkness, the city seems distant, a quasi-civilized frontier outpost, but that is an illusion. El Paso today is isolated by the mind's eye, and little else.

There is a substantial, pervasive history to the place. Up on the hip of Mount Franklin below the mile-high notch called Smuggler's Gap, out on a rocky ledge in the blowing wind and dust, is a seat from which to view the then and now of El Paso.

Below is the city and, without interruption, Juarez. They are gathered across that concrete furrow as one community and have been for 300 years. Beyond Juarez, south into the Mexico desert, is the path of the past.

Conquistadores came from the south, tracking the myths of the seven golden cities: "a galaxy of cities, the inhabitants of which wore civilized raiment, lived in palaces ornamental with sapphires and turquoises, and possessing gold without end," historian Paul Horgan wrote.

Almost a century before the Pilgrims arrived at Plymouth Rock, soldiers of Francisco Vasquez de Coronado rode through the Pass of the North—El Paso del Norte—seeking the rich land of Cibola. A diarist of the period, Pedro de Castaneda, wrote that the Spanish never found their golden cities but, he reasoned with indisputable logic, they "found a place in which to search."

From the mountain overlook, the Rio Grande courses southeast, following an irrigated valley green with truck crops. A field of vegetables there beside the river probably is the longest continuously farmed piece of land in North America.

Far into the distance, those white rumpled nodules on the horizon are the Spanish missions of Ysleta, Texas' oldest community. Once the village was in Mexico but the river's course changed, depositing it in Texas. Founded as the mission Corpus Christi de la Isleta del Sur in 1681, the village at first was a refuge for Tigua Indians, who remained loyal to the Spanish during a general Indian uprising in New Mexico.

Through centuries the Tiguas were absorbed into the white civilization, and by the early 1970s, when the federal government finally recognized them as a tribe, fewer than 100 remained.

With official recognition, establishment of a reservation in El Paso, and the infusion of federal money, the Indians set about to preserve their heritage, constructing an Arts and Crafts Center and restoring early important buildings.

The missions already were ancient when Comanches and Apaches ruled this sandy wilderness, when the Yuma stages passed, when West Texans, with the help of Mexican *vaqueros*, were developing America's cattle industry. That was the real west in its time and El Paso, first known to Texans as Magoffinville—not a name to inspire poetry—was part of it.

For centuries El Paso was alone in this distant nook of Texas, and now its character is neither Texan nor Mexican nor New Mexican nor even American but something else, some special hybrid brand. El Pasoans are an amalgam of all those influences.

The city emits an emotional essence, and it is a town to walk in, get close to.

San Jacinto Plaza, an ancient mid-city square, is a living piece of the past. Once camels from Smyrna, characters of that ignoble experiment in the desert by the U.S. Army, huddled in the plaza as fearful creatures far from home in an alien land. There was a pool of alligators and a large gazebo in which Sunday band concerts were held. Butterfield stages from St. Louis stopped on the plaza before heading west into the badlands nothingness beyond El Paso. Spanish ladies in shawls sold candied Mexican sweets, and there were dandies in scissortail coats dealing open-air three-card monte games.

Nearby the Jackass Mail coaches arrived, and a block farther on, four men died in five seconds of gunfire. A few steps beyond that, John Wesley Hardin, killer of 26 men, expired on the floor of the Acme Saloon, victim of a constable's bullet.

Often I stroll into Hotel Paso del Norte, which dates from the past century, and stare up at the delicate dome of Tiffany glass high above the lobby, an effete touch decidedly out of place in macho El Paso.

But no more anachronistic than the international trolley

that once operated on San Antonio Street. From 1881 and for almost 100 years the streetcars passed back and forth over the Rio Grande to connect El Paso and Juarez, a transportation facility that proved the ease of moving between the two countries. The world's only international trolley, it ceased operations in the 1970s, victim of fiscal difficulties. I miss it.

Today's El Paso still does not have a skyline reflective of its large population. There are few tall buildings and they are dwarfed by the mile-high Franklin Mountains whose flanks rise out of the city. El Paso is wrapped around these mountains and is more compact than most desert communities.

Much is squeezed into the pass—Fort Bliss, a major military facility with historical museums, a zoo, campus of the University of Texas at El Paso. Juarez is over there, replete with all things Mexican—markets, shops, restaurants.

If there is an escape from all this sandy desolation, the heat and the dust, it is north into New Mexico and the high cool forests of Cloudcroft and Ruidoso. El Pasoans go there often. Relief is three hours away.

In all other directions is the desert. East—a long way east on highways flat and straight, built for speed—is Guadalupe National Park, with its McKittrick Canyon, a rare place of America. You can walk into the narrow canyon beside a creek for more than three miles until the trail ends against a rock bluff over which flows a small waterfall. The creek is lined with juniper, madrona, gray oak, fir and maple, the latter a remnant of what once was a great forest of the trees.

There is a variety of honeysuckle in McKittrick not known to grow anywhere else on earth. At one point the southern wall of McKittrick rises almost 2,000 feet to the rear stone shoulders of Pine Top Mountain, a companion to Guadalupe Peak, Texas's highest point, and El Capitan, a great white bold ship's prow of a mountain once the major landmark for wagon trains moving west.

Southeast from El Paso, along the river, drive far enough —to be precise, a mere 323 miles; just a short step out here— and you reach Big Bend National Park, a rough patch of

750,000 remote acres. One thousand square miles of wilderness, of distance and space, of colors washed and muted. The Rio Grande, in the park, is a wild thing coursing through 2,000-foot-high canyons. You can float the white water. And ride horses into the Chisos—the Ghost Mountains—hike on desert trails, explore the stray villages of Candelaria and Ruidoso and Boquillas.

All of this is possible in the grand multi-national foreign state of El Paso. Passports are not needed to visit, though a certain suspension of belief is. The natives are reasonably friendly if somewhat suspect in their choice of home and lifestyle. There is more sunshine than on Mars and enough desert to satisfy anyone's craving for dust and cactus, and a fine crackling air to breathe.

A dose of desert may cure you of everything but homesickness.

1982

PALM SPRINGS: GILT, GLIT AND GRIT

Palm Springs looks like the sort of place where Lawrence of Arabia works in a gas station: an omnipotent sun, tall palms, shifting sand dunes and a spreading desert, flat-roofed cubes of homes, an American Addis Ababa with hot tubs and frozen yogurt.

What a difference a mountain range makes. Back there, west beyond Mount San Jacinto, 105 miles by freeway, is that megalopolic sanitarium, Los Angeles, with its daily snood of smog and movie-set cuteness. Over here, the air is crisp and crackling, dustless. The sun is bright and warm. Nobody complains about the traffic. There are only the backdrop of mountains, the desert, and a lifestyle that makes the Court of Louis XIV seem like the Dukes of Hazzard.

This, as the grandiose claim goes, is "The World's Foremost Year-Round Desert Resort." Maybe. The statistics, to be sure, are grand.

Like 7,000 swimming pools, one for every five residents. And at least 152 tennis courts, nor counting those at private homes. Thirty-four golf courses, which, if you're interested, is 671 holes of golf spread over 107 miles of fairways. And some 200 hotels, motor inns and resorts, but no motels, the richest Indian tribe on earth, hot springs, walnut-stuffed dates, oranges by the bag, 20 canyons for hiking, 1,000-year-old palms, a million or so movie stars who come here to be alone together and, depending on when you take a count, more Rolls Royces than dune buggies.

Palm Springs hardly is your typical small town in rural America.

What it is, is a kind of fantasy village with camels staked out back, a very pleasant lush playground which treats you splendidly if money is no object, and not bad at all if you're the kind who needs to count change.

Palm Springs does have a monied reputation, well-deserved, and a name, also correct, for being warm when the rest of wintering America is wallowing in sleet and snow. That's why incoming jets are filled with emigrants from northern blizzards, many of whom go straight from the plane to the tennis courts and swimming pool, sighing with relief that the Spanish *conquistadores*, Indians and other early desert wanderers, like Hollywood starlets, invented Palm Springs.

Palm Springs is the extravagant, sandy Lazy Susan for Southern California, around which is placed a kind of pseudo-Arabian kingdom speckled by towns with sunny names such as Desert Hot Springs, Thousand Palms, Twenty-nine Palms, Palm Desert, Indio and even the effervescent villages of Oasis, Thermal and Mecca. None of those sandy outposts possesses the glamour and carriage trade of Palm Springs, although Indio is considered the best place in the United States for a fresh date milkshake, if that sort of thing interests you.

Despite its renown as a warm watering hole for celebrities, Palm Springs serves still another function for those who revel in the majesty of the outdoors. It's the center of an immense desert preserve: sand, cactus, high dry mountains, a genuine wilderness in which to wander.

Still, I doubt that many of the million or so annual visitors ever leave pool or golf course or tennis court long enough to trek into the desert surrounding them. They are, after all, here for luxurious escape, not desert escapades. The desert, not air-conditioned, can be uncomfortable.

What has been fashioned for these wealthy vacationers —and make no mistake Palm Springs was developed by and built for the rich and famous—is a smallish town rigidly controlled by its own image. The buildings and homes are low and white and cubed, many imbued with a Moorish style.

A strict architectural code mandates the look of Palm

Springs, down to the restriction that no building may cast a shadow on another, and a ban on billboards, neon, garish signs and even the tacky word, *motel*—there are no motels in Palm Springs, although there are many inns and lodges and villas which we outsiders would mistake for motels (the etymological prohibition creates some difficulty for national chains like, say, Motel 6; the local facility is named Hotel 6).

No denying the austere architectural ordinance has created what appears to be Hollywood's version of a desert sheik's summer camp, but the effect is unexpectedly satisfying to those of us accustomed to the sight of Golden Arches and giant plastic buckets of fried chicken rising over the landscape.

Palm Springs' main street, Palm Canyon Drive, is a splendidly handsome boulevard lined by 1,500 stately palms, all of which are illuminated at night—no common street lights for Palm Springs. Palm Canyon Drive, too, is bordered with expensive and exclusive shops and art galleries and restaurants to serve those film and industrial moguls who double park their Rolls Royces while ordering up another bunch of Gucci loafers.

Because this is a regular retreat for Los Angeles' film colony, the collection of familiar faces changes from hour to hour. You might see anyone: Farrah on this tennis court, Jack Lemmon beside that pool, Carrie Fisher walking her dog on Palm Canyon Drive.

Mostly, though, the celebrities are invisible. Movie stars have a herd instinct. They cluster in and around the half-dozen exclusive clubs and resorts which guarantee privacy. Like the Racquet Club, the intimate enclave that began the Hollywood rush into Palm Springs back in the 1930s. It attracts an older crowd. The younger stars seem to have slipped into the newer Tennis Club and Hotel.

Sundance Villas, a very private huddle of condos, is another star point. Ingleside Inn has been hiding celebrities for three decades (John Travolta and Marlon Brando were in

PALM SPRINGS,
WARM WATERING HOLE
FOR
CELEBRITIES.

J.D. CROWE

residence this winter). La Mancha Private Tennis Club and Villas has high walls and security guards to protect its famous guests.

Nothing keeps you from checking in at these bastions of solitude and seclusion if you can handle the daily rates of about $90 up to, say, the $500 special at Sundance Villas (that rate includes, of course, a private pool and 24-hour chauffeured limousine service).

And there are resident famous faces at Palm Springs. Bob Hope and Sinatra have homes here (each has a street named after him). So does Gerald R. Ford, once a mere U.S. president, and Red Skelton, Danny Thomas and Kirk Douglas.

The salubrious air of Palm Springs indeed is heady stuff, but very democratic. We can breathe it, too. The drawback about rich celebrities is that there are not enough of them to go around. No town can make a living from their patronage alone, and they never seem to be around when you need them.

Thus, the richly embossed reputation of Palm Springs is somewhat of a sham. Its real persona exists in a caviar and cornflakes society. There are as many mobile homes as golf-side chalets. Luxury resorts co-exist with kitchenette rent-by-the-week apartments. As many people play tennis in cut-off jeans as the proper Wimberly whites.

So while Palm Springs may have a posh Racquet Club (which, by the way, is very pleased to have you as a guest, though you may not actually be rich and famous), it also boasts of an Arrowhead Arms Hotel Apartments ($24 daily, winter rates). To balance the elegant Sorrentino's Restaurant (Sinatra celebrated his birthday there the other day), Palm Springs has Hamburger Hamlet (where Sinatra has never celebrated anything). How pretentious can a town really be that peddles Phanny's World Phamous Phudge?

Scrape away the gilt of Palm Springs and you have a friendly little town with a superb climate three seasons of the year, a first-class resort with an endless array of pleasurable activities, and a real desert to explore.

Palm Springs' most salable product is location. With more sunshine than Mars and hardly a cupful of annual rain, the climate is healthy, invigorating. Tucked into the eastern wrinkles of the San Jacinto Mountains, Palm Springs provides scenes of almost awesome natural beauty.

The first visitors, a troop of Spanish explorers in 1744, liked the location and scenery but found the area already settled by Indians living in canyons around natural hot springs. The Spanish called their discovery Agua Caliente or Hot Water. That Indian tribe, today numbering about 180 members, eventually would benefit immensely from their choice of home.

Nothing much happened around Palm Springs until the 1880s when a pair of Los Angeles promoters, one a doctor, purchased land and began touting the area as a prime citrus growing site and the perfect health center. When deep well water was discovered in the 1920s, Palm Springs prospered. Actors Charles Farrell and Ralph Bellamy built the Racquet Club and began luring Hollywoodites to the desert.

And the Indians got rich, largely because of government bureaucratic bungling. In 1891, Congress approved 32,000 acres as a reservation for the Agua Caliente Indians but 50 years passed before a Secretary of the Interior finally approved the lands, much of which in the meantime had become the city of Palm Springs.

In a town where a small corner lot of sand and sagebrush may sell for half a million dollars, the Indians are doing O.K. Many are millionaires. Very quickly, the tribe learned to lease. They also built the Palm Springs Spa, a luxury resort utilizing onetime sacred hot mineral water springs as a health center, sauna, steam and massage complex. The Indians scrub the tourists clean.

The Indians also own and manage Palm and Andreas canyons. You'll pay them a small fee to drive into their canyons. Palm Canyon, especially, is a pleasant spot in which to explore away from town. The canyon is lined with palms, many estimated to be 2,000 years old, that grow no other place in the world. There are hiking trails and a calming stream and pools of spring water.

Andreas is less scenic, but with groves of cottonwood

trees and thickets of wild grapes it is a relaxing place in which to wander.

Out there in the wondrous desert around Palm Springs, all across the Coachella Valley, are millions and millions of acres of wilderness, most of it available for exploring. Center of this arid empire is the Joshua Tree National Monument astride the sandy seam of a pair of grand deserts, the Mojave and the Colorado.

The 850-square-mile preserve was set aside to protect the marvelous Joshua tree, one of nature's better products.

The Joshua, often 40 feet tall, blooms with giant white blossoms in spring, while all around there are bright flowers. These bursts of white and technicolored flowers spread across a beige landscape are a sight of unutterable beauty.

Southward is the unexpected Salton Sea, a natural basin filled in 1905 by flooding waters of the Colorado River. Today, it is a boating, fishing and camping recreational area, and a cool respite amid all that desert.

If the scenery pales, you may explore the Arabic enclave of Indio. Strange little town, the principal industry of which is dates. Millions of pounds of dates. More dates than in any other place in the Western Hemisphere.

That's why restaurants feature dateburgers and date milkshakes, walnut-stuffed dates, candied dates, plain and fancy dates and perhaps, for all I know, even chicken-fried dates. These folks are crazy about dates, living as they do amid a forest of date palms.

To celebrate the popular little fruit, Indio stages a yearly National Date Festival, a kind of country fair for the burnoose set. Chief events of the festival are selection of a date princess and races by ostriches and camels. Seems like innocent fun, although the all-inclusive date syndrome becomes a little oppressive.

There is, for example, a chain of highway signs urging travelers to stop and view a movie titled, *The Romance and Sex Life of the Date.* Is there no decency left?

For all of Palm Springs' natural beauty, its best attraction is man-made, that aerial tramway laid up the face of Mount San Jacinto. You may argue whether nature intended these craggy, rubbly, rocky mountains to be cobwebbed by cable but you may not deny the tram is an engineering miracle and the ride up spectacular.

Just $6.95 buys you a space in the 80-person car for a 2 ½-mile, 18-minute ride up what geologists have determined is the "sheerest mountain face in North America."

On top—at 8,516 feet altitude—is a lodge with restaurant, bar and recreational area and viewing platforms on which to stand and survey the whole of the valley. The view is forever. Below, Palm Springs is a tabletop layout, with its green lawns and golf fairways looking like patches sewn on a beige blanket.

On most days, you can see the Salton Sea in the southern distance and, it is said, on very clear days you can see the dim outline of Las Vegas, far to the north.

Beyond the lodge is the 14,000-acre Mount San Jacinto State Park and Wilderness with campsites, picnic grounds and more than 50 miles of marked hiking trails. In winter, Mount San Jacinto is blanketed with snow, and cross-country skiing is the most popular sport.

Mostly, I think, the tram is best utilized in summer when Palm Springs' weather warms up. When they speak of "mean average temperature" here, nobody tells you how really mean —130 degrees was last summer's high, but the usual average daytime temperature is between 100 and 110 degrees. Everyone is quick to add, "but it is a dry heat," which is supposed to explain everything, but not to me—hot is hot.

To escape the heat everyone seems to stay in the swimming pools, or they go on the tram to the top of Mount San Jacinto where the summer temperature is up to 40 degrees less than down there on the desert floor.

The summer heat does not, however, seem to block the flow of visitors into Palm Springs. People come, anyway, to luxuriate in the shade of the fine little resort town and for a few days of splashing in the pools, playing on the tennis courts and golf courses, and standing on the edge of a splendid desert empire.

It's a nice retreat, this place, even if the dates do have a more interesting sex life than most of us.

1971

FOURTH OF JULY

Once it was Independence Day. Now it is only July
4th. A holiday of sorts, a reason for department store sales,
an office escape plan, a long weekend, leisure time.

It merely is another holiday, which is a mutation of Holy
Day. Independence Day once was a Holy Day, the time for
elation because the Common Man, whatever he is, was given
status and standing almost two centuries ago.

Not that it matters, but they lied to us in the classroom
about Independence Day. They were correct about its effect
but fluffed the cause. The colonists—we—did not, as they
said, pick up a Holy Grail and with God's express permission
and blessing, establish Democracy by divine edict.

God was not involved directly, except perhaps as a disin-
terested onlooker, since He is not known to hang around with
sinners. The Saints of the time mostly were on the other side.

The truth infinitely is more human.

Weather was warm, even hot, that summer in Philadelphia, the colonies' most swinging city, a place of laughter
and music and women. Fine, beautiful, relaxed and consent-
ing women. Delegates came by horseback, early because they
wanted to participate in Philadelphia's excesses.

No one had told them they were assuming a mantle of
greatness. They became great only after our side won and historians made them a little more than they were. Only a few
wanted to separate from England. The Common Man, who
would benefit most from their action, cared not at all about
independence. King George, for them, was a nice guy.

A dirty, foul-smelling Englishman named Tom Paine had
not yet written, "These are the times that try men's souls" but

he had published "Common Sense," a tract that articulated the freedom movement. He sold 120,000 copies in three months and became wealthy, although he still lived in one room.

He really did not even like America, but he appreciated a good fight. Too, he was Franklin's protégé, and old Ben saw the financial benefits of independence for America.

Delegates were a hard-drinking bunch, favoring a concoction of beer and rum, called "flip," and "arrack," a brew of rice and molasses. None of them would touch gin, which was the peasants' drink. They caroused, dipped snuff from silver snuffboxes and most would not sleep in a room with walls covered by paper. Wallpaper, they believed, poisoned sleepers by throwing off a mist of arsenic.

Franklin was a central figure, a kind of Renaissance hippie with shoulder-length hair. He was 5-foot-9 and fat, with a puckish face. His expression always was one of secret amusement. He had an illegitimate son, openly sought out loose women and, lately, had written a hot check or two. But he was brilliant. His eyes were sharp, his forehead high. When thinking, he unconsciously rubbed a mole on his left cheek.

The aristocrats, Washington and Jefferson, stood above the crowd. Washington's pock-marked face, punctuated by dark, sad eyes, did not show his contempt for the freedom movement. Six months earlier he had written that no sane, thinking man wanted independence. Government by the people? He feared that. The Common Man could not be trusted.

Washington was a rich man—mostly because he married the unworldly, silly Martha—but he was in love with the wife of his best friend. He was chosen commander-in-chief of the army, not because he was a proven leader, but because (1) he was rich and (2) he was a southerner and the radicals from Massachusetts needed southern involvement.

John Hancock, vain and lordly, was upset at Washington's selection. He had wanted the job.

Jefferson was the resident intellectual. He spoke the words of Rousseau, Voltaire and Locke and stumped like a revivalist for man's individual rights. But mostly his theories were cerebral, apart from his life. If the noble Jefferson had ever come in contact with the Common Man he served, surely he would have drawn back in disgust.

But, my Lord, how the man could write and it was his eloquence that penned, "When in the course of human events. . . ."

There were others, the Adamses from Boston, the unpopular Samuel, a radical on independence, and his cousin, John, modest and quiet, the man probably most responsible for the rudimentary doctrine of our Constitution. And Patrick Henry of Virginia, gawky and stammering in private but transcended into a hypnotic speaker when thrust onstage— "I am not a Virginian but an American."

The snobbish Jefferson took ideas from John Adams, Franklin, and Washington and drew up the Declaration. The concept was accepted July 2, the day we should be celebrating. But delegates demanded removal of the more radical statements, some of which involved slavery. Slavery was a good business.

The classroom version tells us that on that glorious day in history America's Common Man cheered in the streets and wept with sheer happiness. The truth is most people were depressed and a little upset by the tempestuous document.

Certainly not many of the delegates wanted their names on the paper and it was not until Aug. 19 that John Hancock signed his large, pretentious signature. It was as much as a year later before several of the delegates finally signed.

And when it was over, when this declaration was accepted, the delegates went home. Most were distressed by their deed because they were men trapped by time and place, not the historical giants they became.

And that's the truth. America was separated from England, first by document, then by war. The Common Man won, and His Majesty lost.

It was a simplistic, elegant paper prepared by sinful, frightened men who, unaware, gave us a day away from the office and, coincidentally, changed the course of the world.

A HEAVY TIPPER

1967

A PLAGUE OF TIPPING

W here did we go wrong?

Why do we allow some guy in a red bolero jacket to scowl us into laying out good cash for bad and, often, rude service? What is it about the groveling of our peers in service-business bondage that forces us to scatter our change and sanity?

I'm talking about tipping. It's a plague and one that leaves scars. Any other scourge that visits is immediately pounced on, like, say, the Hong Kong flu, and rendered helpless. Tipping has grown into an almost unmanageable monster. No longer is a gratuity the choice of the giver. Today it is a social and moral obligation.

For anyone who travels regularly tipping is a huge item in the budget. A few years ago I spent the summer in Europe. Tips for the period totaled more than $300. When you figure that today for a little bit more than $300 you can fly to and from Europe then the fact of tips overloading the budget is crushing.

I have paid for my battered luggage thrice over in tips to airport skycaps. Once at Shannon Airport I resolved to be my own carrier and did. But when I attempted to flag down a cab, none stopped. The taxis were halting only for luggage-laden porters.

That's what I call a conspiracy, and I did the only logical thing. I carried my bags back into the terminal, gave them to a skycap, tipped him the equivalent of 50 cents and was allowed to enter a cab.

A friend of mine is a compulsive tipper. Bad service or good, he forks over 15 per cent. He regularly leaves a quarter for a dime cup of coffee. When I ask him why, his explanation never gets past, "Well, I . . ."

Jimmy Durante stayed at Green Oaks Inn in Fort Worth a couple of years ago. He passed around $5 and $10 bills to bellmen for the slightest favor. Asked why, he replied that entertainers have to tip big or they are called cheap.

In theory the system of tipping is that money gifts are given to service employees for good services. Fifteen per cent now is almost standard around the world. And, according to the myth, if service is not good, the tip total is lowered. In practice, however, we all tip regardless.

Psychiatrists tell us that humans accept the tipping plague because we have a need to feel wanted and loved and lack the courage to stare down a rude and incapable waiter.

The thinkers also believe that while service generally has declined in America and tips have remained constant it is because the service people feel insecure in their roles. They give poorer service and extract larger tips to punish the American public.

That is the paradox of tipping. While the practice has spread into a universal institution, service has declined markedly. The New Yorker magazine, possibly in jest, once proposed the "withholding tip" to be deducted from everyone's salary and paid directly to waiters as a subsidy.

Well, tipping, like the poor, seems to be with us always, so ingrained within society that eradication is impossible, if not unthinkable. But reformers have tried.

In 1905, 100,000 Americans banded together as the Anti-Tipping Society. They failed to beat the system. In the early years of this century, six states, Arkansas, Iowa, Mississippi, South Carolina, Tennessee and Washington, passed legislation banning gratuities. The laws were struck down in 1919 as unconstitutional.

A Boston advertising man once formed "Tippers Anonymous," designed not to kill the plague but to equalize it. Members left printed forms—and an appropriate tip—on tables telling waiters whether service had been good, mediocre or atrocious. There were other printed messages for waiters, such as one that said, "Since I am not financially able to tip all people who so graciously serve me, I cannot in fairness single you out to receive an extra gift."

Once there were fake coins imprinted with this message:

"Give nothing. Get nothing. This coin is your tip. It matches exactly the value of your service."

Eleanor Roosevelt felt "the tip has become a wonderful way for the employer to avoid his responsibilities." That is unfair—mostly—to employers, who generally dislike the tipping system. Those who receive the gratuities perpetuate the ritual.

Too many times optimistic employers have tried to eliminate the tip. A New York restaurant once attempted a no tips policy. The public ignored the strategy and tipped anyway. A certain railroad posted "No Tips" signs in their dining cars. The signs soon came down because waiters were telling diners to ignore them and tip anyway, which everybody did.

The petty abuses on the public by tips-collectors are legend and legion. Cab drivers rarely have correct change so they can collect more than the customary tip. In Las Vegas the Maitre d's of hotel lounges routinely place reserved placards on tables for which there are no reservations. To lift this burden you are expected to tip.

If you wonder why cigarette girls and hat check attendants in night clubs wear cute, brief costumes with no pockets, it is because they are not allowed to keep their tips. Concessionaires take the money you think you are giving those leggy females and pay them a flat rate. The pocketless costumes insure the tips are not secreted.

And then there are restroom attendants. Somehow it seems undignified to be attacked in a restroom by a man with a whiskbroom who sweeps away imaginary lint and hands you a towel you could have reached anyway.

The Fort Worth Stock Show probably is the area's worse offender. Each year handicapped persons are posted in restrooms. They do no more than stand by the door to extract an exit bounty from patrons. The system reduces the men to begging and surely more dignified work could be found for them.

Tipping has evolved its own psychology. Those who

know claim scotch drinkers tip more than bourbon sippers. The female martini tippler and the male ginger ale swigger tip small amounts. Tourists are considered poor tippers because, possibly, they don't plan to ever see the waiter, cab driver or porter again.

A survey taken a few years ago showed that Congressmen tip more than Senators but big city mayors tip largest of all. (Most politicians tip larger in an election year.)

The advent of credit cards has chopped into the tip. Business men no longer carry much cash with them. And, as a general rule, smart businessmen don't overtip simply because the tip is deductible and the income tax people are not going to believe a too-large tip.

It has been shown that the man making $10,000 a year spends $400 of it on tips. Jackie Kennedy, according to those movie magazines, tips as much as $25 for a visit to the hairdresser.

Tipping has become so rampant that lateral service people have become addicted. There once was a time when you tipped only a waiter, a cab driver, a barkeep and the telegram delivery boy.

In New York, where tipping has reached critical stages, a friend of mine relates his predicament at Christmas. To come and go at his apartment house in solitude he is expected to lay out approximately two per cent of his yearly rent in Christmas tips to the building's employees.

He hands cash to the doorman, the superintendent, the guy who parks his car, the elevator operator and, strangely, to half-a-dozen others he never sees during the year. The superintendent has been mimeographing suggested cash allowances for himself and others and sliding the tip sheets under the doors.

My friend says if he fails to rise to the occasion he may as well forget about any services for the coming year. In Mexico they call this system the "Mordida," literally "the bite," meaning a bribe to persuade people to do something which they are paid to do anyway.

There seems to be a movement to minimize the indignity of tipping. Tipping, says the theory of recent years, is a fact and should be accepted as such. So, to lessen the shock, 15 per cent automatically is added to your bill and neither party is embarrassed by the passing of filthy money.

Most hotels and restaurants in Europe have adopted the practice of automatic service charge. I subscribe to the method. If a tip is indigenous to service then let it be posted on my bill. The thinking is that service people receive their due, will have a working wage, and service will be excellent. This is the way it should work. I believe this, but then I also accept the fact of Easter Bunnies laying colored eggs each spring.

Probably the service charge eventually will come to American hotels and restaurants as it has to foreign countries. And probably the same thing will happen. In addition to the obligatory service charge, customers will be expected to "add a little bit more."

All travel guides suggest this procedure now. I once checked out of a Madrid Hotel with 12 per cent added to my bill for "service." It still cost me $3.50 to escape. This was spread among maids, floor waiters, bellmen, doormen and parking attendants, all of whom, presumably, were already sharing my 12 per cent.

Tipping is universal, with a couple of major exceptions. Tahiti, that wonderful paradise, accepts no tips. Tips, according to public edict, are enemies to "Tahitian hospitality." In Iceland cab drivers happily drive you around without a thought of your loose change.

Behind the Iron Curtain, the everybody's-equal syndrome had been strengthened by no-tipping legislation. Nonsense. Communist waiters and bellmen take gratuities as readily as their capitalist counterparts.

I once saw a tourism advice sheet for a European country which began, "Tipping has practically been abolished. However, it is customary . . ."

This was to have been a story on tipping advice. Sadly,

there is none available. I undertip, overtip, am bullied into leaving too much for too little, and buy my appreciation and approval with tips. And, undoubtedly, I will continue.

Tipping is a tar baby which we cannot get off our hands. Everybody is stuck.

If you ever are tempted to throw up the whole matter and forgo tipping, I remind you of Judd Gray, a murderer of some reputation a few decades ago. His seemingly was a perfect crime until a cab driver placed him near the murder scene.

The cabdriver remembered Judd because of "a lousy nickel tip."

Mr. Judd probably is the only man ever executed for undertipping, but it should be a lesson for us all.

1980

CITY OF HISTORY, RIVER OF GRACE

Where the San Antonio and Guadalupe Rivers merge is not an important Texas landmark. At their confluence two miles north of Tivoli, a two-cafe village on the coastal plain, the San Antonio is only a pipeline for the larger, more scenic Guadalupe, and its credentials as an essential river are uncertain.

Eastward the newly blended river pokes along for ten miles to enter the Gulf of Mexico at San Antonio Bay, where it pushes a cocoa stain into the blue sea.

The San Antonio is absorbed into the Guadalupe with no evidence of its phlegmatic grace, its episodic history. The stream, in its placid manner, is a Mississippi, a Yangtze, a Nile, and this rag of a river has been fought over, died beside, bled in, blessed, dammed, damned, and doomed.

Sonnets and songs celebrate its epic life. Poet pens acclaim its wandering way. Short stories and novels document its dramatic core. Men have set out for wars from the San Antonio and have come home to it from battles, too often in caskets. It has given love to presidents, shown God to priests. No other unnavigable American river floods across history with the adventuristic style of the San Antonio.

Sidney Lanier, the Georgia poet, once remembered his time with the river, when "memories came whispering down the current."

I understand his emotion for the river but cannot separate the river San Antonio from the city San Antonio, for the two have been one for almost 300 years. They are a single element, fused by time and circumstance. The river is the city's soul, as the Spanish population is its heart and the theatrical history its body. These three inseparable factors are almost seamless in their influence on the city, a gossamer coverlet for the social, cultural, and economic infrastructure that has become modern San Antonio.

The river is best seen from atop the Tower of the Americas, a 750-foot-tall concrete column rising out of HemisFair Plaza, the remaining park of HemisFair '68, the first and only world's fair with a pun in its name. Viewed from the tower's observation deck, the river below is like a lariat thrown carelessly on the ground, with coils and loops and curls, wandering everywhere and nowhere at once. In a mile-long run through the business district the river is crossed by 13 bridges yet has gone no more than 700 straight-line yards.

You cannot escape the river. Cross a bridge, round a corner and there it is again. Because of its river, believed Lanier, San Antonio is "a rare porcupine." Another kind of poet, the star-crossed blues singer, Jimmie Rodgers, said the river calmed his "gypsyfootin'," his "restless heels, soaring wings." Rodgers, the singing brakeman, came to San Antonio in 1924 with a single silver dollar and an ominous cough and until his death never left the city or the river for very long.

John Gunther believed that the city, with its river, was the equal of San Francisco, New Orleans, or Boston as a unique experience, but most outsiders still are startled to find a San Antonio in Texas.

The truth is, it is the state's most comfortable, functional city. If you're rich you make your money in less sensitive markets, like Houston or Dallas or Fort Worth, and you lavish it on San Antonio and the river.

The annual army of marching flowers arrives in San Antonio at the first thought of March to create a bravura of blossoming days. Endemic within the city's spring are pink crepe myrtle, yellow retemas, beds of red cannas, and the white magnolia. The Mexican colors of red and green dominate, and families move into the parks or walk beside the river.

Downtown, within one of its coils, the river winds

through the city at a level 20 feet below the streets, a piece of outdoor sculpture formed with flagstoned walks and exotic plantings. A city park: *Paseo del Río*, the river walk. One spring evening I stepped into the park and strolled the walks, which are lined with cottonwood, bald cypress, willows, wild olive, and palms, and scented by oriental jasmine and new roses and purple sage. The river was busy. A wedding party filled a passing barge, and a water taxi—a *chalupa*—went skimming by. Paddleboats thrashed the water. I sat for a long time near the Commerce Street Bridge, reflecting on the history of that unmagnificent span.

That is where the conquistadores arrived. They came from the south, from across the Rio Grande and the virtually waterless, brushy *brasada*. The San Antonio River held sweet water for the Spanish explorers, who founded the city as the cynosure of a frontier of outpost missions stretching from what would become western Louisiana to Santa Fe.

Later, priests would wade the river at the Commerce Street point, going to their new mission, San Antonio de Valero, known today as the Alamo. Legend has it that the familiar name came from a regiment of Mexican soldiers who were quartered there so long, 11 years, that they began calling themselves *los álamos*, after the cottonwoods growing along the riverbanks. In 1736 a temporary footbridge—six large beams—was laid but ultimately removed because the wooden span became a handy access route for attacking Indians. By 1836 a plain yet strategically important footbridge had been built, and the city's defenders retreated across it to the Alamo and martyrdom. After the fort's fall, Santa Anna traversed the bridge to inspect his victory.

Over the years many notable visitors have written of the charm, the mystique of the Commerce Street Bridge. Frederick Law Olmsted, creator of New York City's Central Park, walked the bridge in the 1850s, writing later that the river flowed "rapidly but noiselessly." Lanier, by 1872 consumptive and dying, stood on the bridge and described "the green translucent stream flowing beneath." O. Henry, in his story, "A Fog in San Antone," wrote of his tubercular victim on a "little iron bridge . . . under which the small tortuous river flows." And it probably was the Commerce Street Bridge from which author Stephen Crane once leaped to save a drowning child.

In San Antonio, everyone comes to the river. A young Army lieutenant named Ike and his sweetheart, Mamie, held hands as they walked the riverbanks, bound for a Mexican dinner at the Original Cafe.

Another Army officer, Douglas MacArthur, came there regularly, as did a newly commissioned flier named Lindbergh; a mustached Teddy Roosevelt and, years later, his cousin Franklin; a tank commander called Patton; that old carouser and whiskey drinker Ulysses S. Grant; and a sag-eyed, stoop-shouldered small man named Robert E. Lee.

Lyndon Johnson and Lady Bird married in a nearby Episcopal church—with license No. 105133—and afterwards strolled over the bridge and to the river.

Today the river loop, the park, is lined with shops, good restaurants, and night clubs and is the center of all that occurs in San Antonio, from outdoor art shows that may attract 250,000 people on a sunny spring afternoon, to Fiesta, a week-long celebration each April of parades and costume balls and more than a little Spanish pomp and circumstance to celebrate the city's Hispanic heart.

No American city is more Spanish than San Antonio—it has five Spanish missions, four Spanish plazas, more Spanish-speaking, Spanish-surnamed people than Veracruz, Puebla, or San Luis Potosi, Mexico. Several radio and television stations broadcast solely in Spanish. In Market Square, one of those ancient plazas, there are shops of herb doctors—the *curanderos*—where potions of ground deer horn—*cuerno de venado*—and concoctions of sunflower seeds and kidney weed and creosote bush may be purchased. The San Antonio Yellow Pages even has a listing for "midwifery."

The Spanish of course came first, but San Antonio always has been a gathering place and crossroads of early America. Ethnic legacies abound. St. Patrick's Day has been stretched into a week-long celebration on the river, more often than not with the water tinted shamrock green. Each Sunday, the Chinese Baptist Church conducts sermons in two languages—English and Mandarin. The 50-voice Beethoven Männerchor has been singing classical German music for more than 100 years. There is an annual Greek festival and a Lebanese fair complete with San Antonio-born belly dancers. Each August, the Texas Folklife Festival, one of the state's largest annual events, brings together more than 30 ethnic groups for an orgy of foods and music.

San Antonio has been called an ethnic gumbo, although the basic spice always is Spanish. Two hundred years of community togetherness has intermingled ethnic origins to the extent that there are families named O'Brien whose forefathers lived in the Canary Islands, blond-haired teutonic Garzas, and a Gonzales clan with relatives in Glasgow.

All of these multi-national influences have been part of an adventurous history of no small measure. Still remembered is the sight of Sunday dudes and their ladies riding ostriches in the parks. And a classic battle staged between a lioness and Mexican fighting bull (the bull won). And the Buckhorn Saloon, where cowboys were permitted to ride their horses up to the bar. In about 1868, an unknown hero employed at Marnisch Baer's confectionery shop invented the ice cream soda (the claim is disputed, but I choose to believe San Antonio's version). San Antonio is the city that invented that most palatable of Texas soul foods—chili. And in San Antonio O. Henry invented an enduring western character, the Cisco Kid.

San Antonio is an uncommon place.

Not surprisingly, San Antonio's early planners did not anticipate the automobile. Many streets follow paths of old water ditches—the *acequias*—which nourished the early mission families who clustered around the traditional village squares. The city's downtown streets would more fittingly accommodate oxcarts and horses, and today those Spanish plazas are best reached by foot. Although of all of San Antonio's ancient squares, Alamo Plaza is the least attractive today, a walking tour of the city should begin there because, truthfully, San Antonio—and modern Texas—begin at the Alamo.

The plaza has become a major thoroughfare for city traffic, and only after dark, when the automobiles have gone, does the magic of yesteryear return, recalling a time when the square was bustling with withered old women in black mantillas hawking boutonnieres and thin Mexican candies, German burghers seeking a favorite beer garden, and intemperate cowboys firing off their pistols for the pure hell of it.

Facing Alamo Plaza the Menger Hotel still stands as it has for more than 120 years. In a corner of the lobby, before a giant fireplace, William Sidney Porter scratched short stories on long yellow pads. Only after he left San Antonio, having served a jail term for embezzling $554.48 from an Austin bank, did he become famous as O. Henry, remembering the city in seven of his stories, and Texas in two dozen others.

Oscar Wilde, dressed in yellow silk waistcoat, blue tie, green cape, and black breeches, fed raw meat to alligators living in a patio pool at the Menger. Cattlemen headquartered in the Menger. Richard King, owner of the sprawling King Ranch, often rode the 20 miles from his house to the ranch's front gate, then boarded a stagecoach to San Antonio to meet his friend, Shanghai Pierce, another cattleman, at the Menger.

The hotel's European-trained kitchen staff brought forth specialties like *Grouse Farci aux Truffes* and *Cailles en Aspic*, and from the wine cellar, *Duc de Reichstadt* champagne. King and Pierce, though, preferred more local fare such as buffalo hump roast, wild turkey, deer loin—and turtle steak fresh from the San Antonio River.

Lee and Grant, FDR, generals Patton, Pershing, Zachary Taylor, and William Tecumseh Sherman, writers Bret Harte and Joaquin Miller, capitalist Jay Gould, frontiersmen Buffalo Bill Cody and Sam Houston, actresses Anna Held and Sarah Bernhardt—all trod the marble-floored lobby during the Menger's halcyon years.

Teddy Roosevelt stopped at the Menger when he arrived

in San Antonio to form his Rough Riders—the first U.S. Volunteer Cavalry of the Spanish-American War. Mostly they were young San Antonians, but West Texas cowboys signed up, too, men with strange names like "Sore-eyed Bill" and "Shirt-collar Sam." There were others, such as William Tiffany of the Fifth Avenue Tiffanys and Hamilton Fish, Jr., termed a "millionaire playboy," who lined up at the Menger's bar—still in use today—to become Rough Riders. Each had to swear he was "entirely sober when enlisted."

Next door to the Menger is the Alamo, Texas's best-known shrine. Trouble had been brewing for over a year when 187 men died there in 1836, at the hands of Santa Anna and his vast army. By 1835, the desire of some Texans for independence from Mexico had led to armed revolt and a series of military confrontations. On December 9, Texas rebels took San Antonio from the Mexican forces garrisoned there. It was to put down these insurgents that dictator Antonio Lopez de Santa Anna marched his armies north across the Rio Grande.

The 104 men who were left to defend San Antonio knew that they faced nearly insurmountable odds. As they withdrew to fight from behind the walls of the Alamo, William Travis, co-commander with James Bowie, issued a plea for aid "with all dispatch." Sam Houston, who was engaged with Mexican troops near Goliad, 100 miles away, sent 30 men, all he could spare. Soon they were joined by a small band of reinforcements led by Tennessean Davy Crockett. Thirty more slipped through enemy lines from Gonzales.

The heroes came from varied backgrounds. Only a handful were native Texans. Most were adventurers from the United States who shared the Texans' desire for self-government. Thirty-six were English and the others included Scots, Irish, two Germans, and a Dane. Only six had been in Texas for as long as five months. Few were literate. It is unlikely that more than half of them could have read the Texas Declaration of Independence which was adopted, unbeknownst to them, at the Constitutional Convention four days before their defeat on March 6.

Historian Ed Syers believed that until the last the men never really thought they would die there. Travis was not, Syers wrote, "oriented toward martyrism."

But Travis' message to the people of Texas, containing the words, "I am besieged. . . . I shall never surrender or retreat," is one of the great documents of courage in history.

The men died fighting inside the stone and adobe walls. Santa Anna, who considered himself the equal of Napoleon, prolonged the final attack with bittersweet tactics. He alternately had marksmen fire on the Texans, then followed with classical music played by his regimental band. Santa Anna's strength was in masses of men, and on the 13th day of siege, when he raised the red flag of no quarter and commanded his trumpeters to sound the chilling *degüello*, 2,000 Mexican soldiers swarmed over the Alamo's walls, and a legend was born.

"Remember the Alamo!" first was heard little more than a month later, when Sam Houston's soldiers, seeking to avenge the martyrs and win independence, surprised and overran Santa Anna's army at San Jacinto. In 1849, the first U.S. Army garrison arrived in San Antonio to restore the Alamo. Today the city is headquarters of the Fourth U.S. Army and houses large numbers of military personnel at Fort Sam Houston, Randolph Field, Kelly Field, and Lackland Air Force Base, also a medical center of renown.

Military Plaza, across the river, is less special historically than Alamo Plaza but more typical of San Antonio. It was a military compound as early as 1731 and later an outdoor market where citizens bargained for vegetables, hens for Sunday dinners, fiery bowls of chili, mockingbirds in wicker cages, buffalo hides, and donkeys. Some people also had teeth pulled alfresco by itinerant dentists; others had their pockets picked; some were shot by cowboys or hanged by vigilantes.

A magnificent oak once stood at the plaza's southeast corner. It was called the "Law of Mondragon," named for a vigilante leader. It was a hanging tree, about which was composed a ballad containing these words:

The Law of Mondragon
All Texans will endorse
That here in San Antone
You must not steal a horse.

The last vestige of Military Plaza's past is in the Spanish Governors' Palace. Neither a palace nor occupied by governors, it was the residence of the ranking emissary of the King of Spain. The mustard-colored structure is the last remaining example in Texas of an aristocratic Spanish house. Fully restored, the low-profiled home was built in 1749. It is furnished with period artifacts, including carved canopy beds covered by gold damask cloth and tooled leather chairs in the *sala*—a room for entertaining.

Main Plaza—*Plaza Principal de Bexar*—should be seen at dawn. In the civil twilight of a spring morning, the sounds of the bells of San Fernando Cathedral fill the square, along with the smells of coffee and frying bacon, and the special aroma of tortillas from nearby cafes.

San Fernando Cathedral has stood in the plaza for two and a half centuries. On exceptionally clear mornings sunlight forms an aureole above the cathedral's bell towers, each of which is crowned by a white cross.

To see the reflected halo you must stand on the steps of a Gothic redstone courthouse south of the church. There is only a brief moment when the effulgence of light sprays the towers, but it is a remarkable sight and one that has been repeated for centuries, during which a lengthy melodrama of history has played below.

In 1749, Apaches came to settle a peace with Spain. The treaty—soon broken—was consummated in the plaza with the ritualistic burial of a live horse, a tomahawk, a lance, and six arrows. Those peace tokens still are there, now under the grounds of a small green park. In front of San Fernando in 1813, the American Volunteers made North America's first declaration of independence from Spain. Years later, Davy Crockett stood on a wooden box in this square to speak in his backwoodsy, mesmeric style to men who were destined to die at the Alamo. In a hotel across the plaza, a troubled Robert E. Lee paced away the night agonizing over personal loyalties. By sunrise on that day in 1861, he had decided to join the Confederacy.

Not within walking distance of downtown but still beside the river are San Antonio's Spanish missions: San Juan Capistrano, Concepción, San Francisco de la Espada, and San Jose, a natural historic site and a magnificent architectural psalm in stone and mortar.

Many different events led to the creation of San Antonio, a city in the path of history and time and geography. But today, realistically, the river cannot live except by municipal support, much as civic patrons support an opera company or a symphony orchestra.

San Antonio is located on the southern edge of the Edwards Plateau and a geological aberration, the Balcones Fault, a series of underground vaults created by slippage of rock strata. Rainwater flows from Edwards Plateau into the limestone vaults. North of San Antonio this water flow is shaped much like a candelabra, its upraised arms representing tributaries, and the San Antonio River, the spine. Once the river flowed from a gushing spring, and the spring water flooded the river throughout its 180-mile run to the Gulf of Mexico. But the springs long ago were siphoned from their limestone caverns for industrial and residential use.

Today the San Antonio River Authority controls the river's use and fixes its rate of flow, pumping 879,000,000 gallons of well water annually into the streambed from a large brown pipe in Brackenridge Park, the city's central green space.

Regardless of its source, the San Antonio remains a nurturing parent, though the civilization it has nourished is perhaps not one ranking with that of the Euphrates or the Brahmaputra. It is a thin stream, shallow and unpretentious, yet there is in its pure, milky green water a charismatic splendor no one ever can adequately explain.

1979

TEXANS IN NEW YORK

Ah, New York City of the solicitous possible dream. Naked city of promise, the martyred megalopolis of metaphysical malfeasance.

New York: Metaphor for the warp and woof of America. Vast, flawed, brash, impersonal, unfriendly and friendless, corrupt and possibly obsolete and probably irretrievably bankrupt.

The place of seven million jostled strangers, immigrant passengers hunkered in their little concrete boxes being hurtled into a future that does not exist.

What is New York City made of? Dogdoo-smeared sidewalks, malevolent muggers, three income taxes, acrimonious taxi drivers for whom the shortest distance between two points is against their principles, and a pack of nativeborn cynics who suspect a cheery "Good morning."

Somehow it is anti-American, and quite probably psychoneurotic. And ethnic groups. New York is an alphabet soup of congregated foreigners from Abyssinians to Zanzabarians. Indeed a multinational city, New York has more Italians than Naples, more Irish than Shannon, more Puerto Ricans than Ponce, more Jamaicans than Port Antonio and more Texans than Tyler.

So, there are seven million stories in the naked city and this is perhaps 100,000 of them, more or less, even though you can't find a decent chicken fried steak in the whole place.

Texans, of course, are an ethnic group. They are here, these Texans, as missionaries of sanity amid madness, strewn among savages who eat their beef bloodrare, hardly ever say "ma'am" to women and think enchilada is a town in Southern California.

Texans always have been in New York but never have they been so numerous and visible and influential as they are today. It is only my theory—a valid one, I believe, that the ascension of Texanism in New York closely parallels New York's recovery from near-fatal bankruptcy. As New York has rebounded with unusual vigor, Texanism is rife. It just may be that the dose of Texanism saved New York, though New York seems largely ungrateful about it all.

A delegation from the Hill Country hamlet of Luckenbach arrived in New York last fall to advise the city in its time of fiscal crisis. Among their suggestions, Luckenbachians asked the U.S. Department of Agriculture for a subsidy not to grow tobacco in Manhattan and asked Mayor Edward Koch to start an egg route. "Why, he could make maybe $300 a week on them eggs," a Luckenbachian explained.

Mayor Koch and New York were unimpressed. Last month Koch turned down a hand-delivered key to the city of Dallas, but perhaps he is still peeved about American Airlines returning its headquarters to Texas.

The permeation of Texanism into the lifestyle of New York is an amazing phenomenon, not altogether caused by the Texans who live here. Whatever the complete reason for this Texas thing is unimportant. Just understand that Texas is an idea whose time has come in New York.

One recent Sunday my bags and I were delivered to a New York Hilton cubicle. I switched on the TV. The Dallas Cowboys were playing football, between commercials by Bob Lilly showing us how to build doghouses without sawing off fingers and Roger Staubach selling men's clothes for a New York store.

The New York telephone book assays the Texas business life in the big city. More than 50 entries, from Texas Agri-Science Inc. to Texas Trading and Milling Corp. to Texas Boat Company to Texas Color Printers Inc. to Texas International Drilling Fund to Texas Pacific Land Trust to Texas Pipe Bending Company to Texas Sunday Comics Section Inc. to Texas Tour Service.

If I had chosen, I could have dined on Texas Fried Chicken or Texas Taco. I could find real Mexican food at Anita's Chili Parlor, or chicken and dumplings at Summerhouse, a restaurant co-owned by June Jenkins, the wife of writer Dan Jenkins. There's also the New York Texan and the Lone Star Cafe and Wick Fowler's 2-Alarm Chili.

After the football game, Texan Dan Rather appeared as one of three reporters on CBS' "60 Minutes." Later, I could have selected several kinds of Texas-influenced entertainment. "The Fantasticks," written by a pair of Texans, has been playing for 18 years off-Broadway. "Vanities," by Corsicana playwright Jack Heifner, is another off-Broadway hit. On Broadway, "The Best Little Whorehouse in Texas" is a smash hit written, directed, choreographed and performed by Texans. Kinky Friedman, known as the "Texas Jewboy," was picking and singing at the Lone Star Cafe.

I know all of this because New York Magazine, edited by Texan Joe Armstrong, fully documents the Texan influence on the big city. There are Texans all over the masthead of "Rolling Stone" and "The Village Voice." And movie critic Rex Reed, a native Texan, was explaining a nuance or two about other Broadway shows.

A full-page ad in the New York Times depicted a Texas-dressed cowboy strolling across Wall Street. It was selling western clothes—"gear"—for The Chelsea Corral. Later, as I took an evening stroll, I passed a department store window filled with more westernwear—three lady manikins dressed in big hats, Texas boots and fringed skirts, the way Warner Brothers dressed its starlets for western pictures in the 1940s. It seems that interpretation of the Texas image almost always is wrong when practiced by unknowledgeable New Yorkers.

And that's just the Sunday Texas lineup.

Historically, this Texans-in-New-York thing had its beginnings perhaps as far back as the 1880s when a San Antonio cowboy shot out gaslights on Broadway to impress a lady friend, then fought six cops to a standstill. Shanghai Pierce, a South Texas rancher, once settled his elbows onto a New York bar top and ordered himself some whiskey. Moments later he stormed out of the saloon, shouting to friends.

CAN YOU SPOT THE TEXAN?

N THIS NEW YORK CROWD?

"Why, they're charging four-bits a swaller in that damned place."

When Buffalo Bill's Wild West Show and later the Madison Square Garden Rodeo began calling annually on New York, Texans by the score roared into the Big Apple. There is a story about the Texas rodeo performer who galloped his horse through the lobby of the Waldorf Astoria and another who sneaked his horse into a hotel suite, then attempted to order a bale of hay from room service.

During Prohibition, Texas Guinan's speakeasy was the most popular in New York. The little Texas lady always greeted her customers with a "Hello, Suckers," and they were. Tex Rickard, the promoter, once fielded a sports team named the Rangers. He passed the players off as being actual descendents of real Texas Rangers, although they were from more prosaic places such as Hackensack, N.J. and Millomina, Ill.

Old Amon Carter began coming to New York regularly in the 1920s and for three decades performed as the superlative Texan. Dressed in his purple and white (TCU colors) boots, a large-crowned cowboy hat, a diamond stickpin in his kerchief and sometimes a pair of twin pearl-handled pistols. Amon strutted through the town hollering "Yippee" to everyone, using that put-on twangy Texas voice and generally consolidating New Yorkers' beliefs that Texans are larger than life. He once drove a stagecoach down Wall Street and he paraded with bands and fired off his pistols to start bicycle races.

Throughout all of this Texan-in-New-York history, a peculiar recurring theme emerges. Texans in New York are more Texan than in Texas. "Playing Cowboy" is what writer Larry King calls it. They exaggerate all the Texas mannerisms and act out the myths for gullible New Yorkers.

Amon Carter was a hard-headed businessman, now a cowboy, with a normal speaking voice except when he was playing professional Texan. "Larry (King) has lived in Washington and New York twenty years," says a friend, "and he still sounds like he just jumped the fence in West Texas."

The Texas Cowboy syndrome is why sports writer and

author Dan Jenkins says he lives on "5th Street"—actually the elegant Fifth Avenue, and why syndicated columnist Liz Smith served her New York guests chicken fried steak with the option of drinking either Dom Perignon champagne or Dr Pepper, and why Leigh Curry, an investment broker from Sweetwater, has imbedded his collection of rattlesnake skins, fangs and rattlers in a clear lucite toilet seat in his Greenwich Village apartment, and why Women's Wear Daily's sophisticated Rosemary Kent was married wearing her chili pepper red boots with bridesmaids dressed as "wranglerettes" carrying cactus bouquets, and why New York Magazine Editor Joe Armstrong wears a cowboy shirt he claims once belonged to Roy Rogers. It goes on.

Playing Cowboy. New Yorkers, as provincial and naive as a village of Yemenite date farmers, are ever fascinated by the prairie patois of Texans, by Texans' gregarious personalities. "They almost prefer that you not be able to read or write," mused one Texan embroiled in the New York experience.

The rise of Texanism in New York benefits from the entire western-style revolution of the 1970s where clothing is adapted to the sleek western casualness. Jeans became haute couture, whether in a Manhattan restaurant or on the streets of Laredo. Country-Western music, especially the Austin-inspired sounds, became a wave engulfing all forms of entertainment.

What you have in New York are guys dressed like ranch hands from Lubbock, complete with rough-out boots and sweat-darkened Stetsons drinking Lone Star Beer—complete Texans until, says one observer. "They open their mouths and out come those Bronx accents." And what you have are Texans everywhere, being Texan.

Before this pop western explosion, back in and after the LBJ days when Texans were considered crude rubes, there were closet Texans all over New York. "They spent years trying to remove the edges from the way they talked and acted," the observer said. Now, they can talk Texas again, and act Texas without being ashamed of their roots.

New York, for all of its tribulations and disadvantages—

and they seemingly are without end—remains an exciting, dramatic city, center of America's arts and entertainment, business and banking. If you have made it to the top in New York, you have climbed the Mount Everest of world cities. And those visible Texans in New York have made it, or are making it.

There seems no place in New York untouched by Texan hands. Like CBS. A few years ago, all major CBS news shows were anchored by Texans. Walter Cronkite, a University of Texas graduate, still anchors the major 6 o'clock news. Dan Rather has moved on to "60 Minutes."

Bob Schieffer, the former *Star-Telegram* reporter, has arrived to anchor CBS' morning news show. "You almost have to have the right accent to get hired around here," Schieffer said. When he arrived, the show staff presented him with a gift—a bottle of long neck Lone Star Beer.

Hughes Rudd, a Waco native, still does news commentaries and concocts the best bowl of chili in town. "When Hughes gets a cold, he immediately makes chili. He thinks it cures anything," Schieffer said.

It is no doubt the challenge of New York that lures Texans up here. "New York is a frontier and Texans still have a frontier mentality," explains Fort Worth attorney Kirk Purcell, who sometimes entertains in the Lone Star Cafe. "In New York, I find myself feeding on the energy of the street craziness, the energy of the whole place. I have a great deal of respect for the people who make their living out of the sheer creativity of New York."

New Yorkers and Texans are more alike than either would like to admit. "It takes some adjustment to the pace," explains former Dallasite Barbara Taylor, who runs her own public relations agency. "When you get the pace down, it's alright. You can compete. New Yorkers and Texans both are aggressive."

"Texans seem to thrive in New York in a way other outlanders don't," said Sam Scott Miller, senior vice president and general counsel for Paine Webber. "People from the Midwest seem to perceive it as a balancing act." Miller arrived in

New York out of Fort Worth via Yale with his Mississippi wife and noticed immediately that southerners, "especially Texans, take to New York and enjoy it more than any others I've seen."

It is this adjustment of horizontal upbringing to vertical environment that separates Texans from all the others. Two secretaries from Des Moines may huddle in their one-room efficiency for years but Texans are out on the streets "The Texans here tend to be visible," claims Dan Jenkins. "They just overpower everybody."

Consider, for example, Judy Buie. She is cute, blonde, pert and perky, from Itasca, a TCU graduate in film, former promotion writer for 20th Century Fox and CBS, a freelance photographer and seller of Texas boots.

The east 60s area of New York City is a ritzy neighborhood in which society matrons walk their snooty little French poodles and 10-table restaurants abound. It's fashionable and fancy. Serendipity is a restaurant-boutique next door to the French Jean Store (customers are invited to lie down while attempting to pull on the tight French jeans). Past the cash register and up the stairs is Judy Buie's boot shop, called merely "Texas."

It is nothing but stacks of boot boxes, a set of steerhorns, a coiled rattlesnake ashtray, a bench, Willie singing on the stereo and Ms. Buie. Her shop is the only real Texas cowboy boot store in New York and success was instantaneous.

Like most good ideas, it came accidentally. Buie wore boots on photography assignments. People kept asking her to bring them a pair next time she was in Texas. So many people asked that she decided to open the boot shop. She has tripled her stock in two years.

Andy Warhol bought a pair (green). Actress Catherine Deneuve ordered a $600 pair of ringtail lizard boots. Lola Redford, Robert Redford's wife, wears Judy Buie boots. So does pro basketball star Walt Frazier.

New Yorkers, being New Yorkers, will not settle for plain boots. Colors—green and red, especially—are big sellers, and exotic skins. "Iguana skin is a big seller to people who don't know what an iguana is," said Buie. "The gays tend to buy the brighter colors, the straights are more conservative."

Her publicity days with CBS and 20th Century were not wasted. Ms. Buie knows how to promote her shop and herself. The most successful was a "I'm wearing Texas cowboy boots with . . ." party staged in the Lone Star Cafe. Guests were encouraged to wear their boots with fantasy outfits, to the delight of major New York newspapers and television stations who covered the event.

Guests arrived wearing Texas boots and a bikini. Boots and an Yves St. Laurent tuxedo. Boots and long johns. Boots and a floor length lynx cape. Boots and an antique wedding dress. Boots and a $5,000 chiffon dress from Georgio Sant'Angelo. Boots and a plastic transparent motorcycle jacket.

Willie Woo, a jewelry designer, wore his custom made boots with jeans and a pony tail. Another guy wore boots and a gold jock strap. Two men arrived in boots, announcing, "We're Fred and Terry . . . just a couple of cowboys."

The New York Times reported the party was a "chili-in-paper cups wang-dang," whatever that is.

The important thing about all of this feeding of the "Midnight Cowboy" syndrome is that Judy Buie sold more Texas boots, and advanced the cause of Texanism in New York.

Tommy Tune, who is six-feet-six-inches tall and slender as a fence post, arrived for Judy Buie's party wearing leather chaps and boots on his hands—his were too small for his feet.

Tune, born in Wichita Falls and raised in Houston, is a dancer, good enough to win a Tony—Broadway's Oscar—for his work in the musical "Seesaw" and the Obie Award for an off-Broadway musical called "The Club."

"There are a lot of similarities between Texans and New Yorkers," Tune says.

He cites his current success as proof—"The Best Little Whorehouse in Texas." He is co-director with fellow Texan Peter Masterson, and he staged the musical numbers. "I wasn't aware of all the Texans in New York until I began working on 'Whorehouse,' and then they began coming out of the woodwork," Tune says.

"Whorehouse" is the story of LaGrange's Chicken Ranch, the brothel that existed for more than 140 years before it was shut down this decade by Dolph Briscoe. The show is filled with Texans and Texanisms and is an overwhelming success on Broadway where New York audiences probably do not understand either the language or the Texas subtleties concocted by author Larry King, a native West Texan.

Masterson, a native of Angleton and a graduate of Rice University, has a long list of acting credits from Broadway's "The Championship Season" to Hollywood's "The Stepford Wives."

"Texans," says Tune, "had first crack at the roles. They didn't have to learn the language." Carlin Glynn, who plays Mona, the madam, is from Houston. J. Frank Lucas is a TCU graduate. Susan Mansur attended Abilene Christian College. Those are the major roles taken by Texans.

King's voice is heard as halftime announcer for a scene showing a group of dancing girls similar to the Kilgore Rangerettes performing for a Texas Aggie football crowd. Carol Hall, still another Texan, wrote the words and music, both of which won her this year's Drama Desk Awards.

"Whorehouse" came from an article King wrote for *Playboy*. He and Masterson adapted it for an Actors' Studio project, then opened off-Broadway before moving it into the Broadway theater last summer.

"I'm really not into the Texan thing," says Masterson. "I mean I don't go around wearing boots and talking Texas. I don't play Texan. Well, I do have an annual San Jacinto Day party. I invite all the Texans I know and then everybody I know who hates Texas. That makes a good mix. And two Mexicans. I think a San Jacinto Day party needs two Mexicans."

You won't believe this but it's true. A New York taxi driver once ran over a Tibetan yak. The yak is a big furry beast that looks like a shaggy Holstein. As news stories described the animal, it stood six feet tall at the shoulders, weighed 1,200 pounds and was wandering through dark Bronx streets after escaping from the zoo. The taxicab bolted into the night and struck the yak broadside. The yak keeled over dead. The driver bloodied his head on the windshield. The cab was demolished.

Out of the rear seat stepped the taxi's lone passenger, a Texan, properly booted and hatted, wearing jeans and a woolly sheepskin rough-out jacket. He looked at the dead yak and rushed for help in the nearest saloon where he blurted to the bartender, "Gawdamighty, we just killed the hairiest cow I ever saw."

Later, according to the old *New York Mirror*, the Texan explained to newsmen, "Well, I'll tell you one thing, it almost scared me to death, and I ain't just awoofin' you." Newsmen ignored the yak. They had found a stranger animal. A real live Texan.

Which brings us to Rudolph, the Red-Nosed Iguana.

The iguana is a monumental symbol of Texanism in New York, crouched on the roof of the Lone Star Cafe, a kind of halfway house for incoming Texans trying to adjust to the city and, at all times, a country-western-chili-beer haven for homesick Texans.

In a town where crazies stroll around naked or wearing Batman suits and nobody even glances at them, the iguana on lower Fifth Avenue has drawn considerable attention, not the least of which came from the Fifth Avenue Association, which at first thought the thing was some kind of transcendental medieval dragon.

Yet there it squats on the Lone Star's roof, as though to pounce on passing buses. It's 40 feet long, has green scaly-skin and an illuminated tongue. At Christmas, the plastic beast was outfitted in antlers and a bright red nose—thus the name: Rudolph the Red-Nosed Iguana.

Rudolph was sculpted with urethane foam on a wire and steel skeleton by Bob Wade, a Texas artist now based in New York who conducts his art business from the Lone Star Cafe. Wade, who taught art at North Texas State University for four years, first made headlines with his football-field size map of the United States that he constructed in 1976 with a grant from the National Endowment for the Arts.

Last year he designed and transported to Paris a customized Airstream trailer for the Biennale in the Museum of Modern Art. The trailer became a "Texana Museum" complete with a stuffed horse from Fort Worth's Museum of Science and History.

The iguana was sculpted first for Artpark, a program of the National Heritage Trust, and was erected near Niagara Falls.

Wade later decided to move his iguana to New York City and contacted Lone Star Cafe owner Mort Cooperman, who agreed to mount the reptile at his restaurant. He and an assistant dismantled the iguana, packed it into a U-Haul Truck (except the head, which was tied on top), and zoomed down to New York City, arriving at 4 a.m.

Almost immediately, two big guys tried to steal the head (New York muggers will attack anything, even a 40-foot-iguana head). Later in the day, a crane lifted the iguana into place. The Fifth Avenue Association soon branded the plastic sculpture as "too outrageous."

Wade does not know what art project he will do next. He has given up the idea of a 75-foot-long inflatable iguana because of the expense. Perhaps a huge pair of Texas boots . . . "or maybe," he says thoughtfully, "a giant praying mantis."

A few New Yorkers thought the iguana was a dragon. Others confused it with an armadillo. But none of these mistakes really disturb Cooperman, whose Lone Star Cafe is becoming one of the most photographed landmarks in New York.

It is a nondescript place, except for the iguana and the large sign above the revolving door: "Too Much Ain't Enough." The cafe's major advertising slogan touts it as the "Best Honky-Tonk North of Abilene."

It isn't really the best, but it is a reasonable facsimile of a Texas beer joint. Cooperman, a non-Texan who grew up liking country-western music, was an advertising man weary of his trade. He visited Texas for several clients, and the Texanism seed was planted.

One day he was driving from Connecticut to New York.

He had a headache and parked on the side of the road to rest. He turned on the radio to a country-western station and it soothed his pained head. Then and there, he decided to open a beer joint.

The result has been astounding, if for no other reason than he sells 20,000 bottles of long neck Lone Star Beer every month at $2 a pop.

Thirteenth Street and Fifth Avenue, on the edge of Greenwich Village, is a good spot for a hole-in-the-wall beer joint. It is a narrow place with tiny tables jammed together. Through the revolving door, the bar is old-fashioned and festooned with Texanisms—signs blaring "Long Live Longnecks" and "Honk if you love Willie Nelson" and "Everybody's Somebody in Luckenbach." There are huge plastic Lone Star bottles and a Dallas Cowboy cheerleaders' poster.

I joined the crowd there for lunch one day. There were secretaries and men dressed in Wall Street suits and shoppers killing an hour. The one-sheet menu features chili and hamburgers. The chili was so-so, but New Yorkers wouldn't know the difference because most of them were pouring ketchup over it. No one was crumbling crackers, which proved there were few Texans in the place.

"I couldn't exist solely on Texans," Cooperman admitted. "But lots of New Yorkers seem to like us."

That's true. One recent Sunday night, at least 300 people jammed the cafe. The attraction was Kinky Friedman, the Texas Jewboy from Kerrville, who now lives on Long Island.

Fort Worth attorney Purcell was warming up the audience with his stage character, the Rev. Billy Joe Bob Sweeney, a fundamentalist preacher.

Wrapped in an American flag, the Rev. Sweeney told of how he and Kinky graduated from the San Diablo Bible College in Del Rio, with degrees in theology and welding and storm door repair.

Purcell concocted his preacher character as a satire on the hypocrisy of Southern Baptists when he was a student at Baylor Law School. It is an impersonation real enough to cause some New Yorkers to wonder if he really is a preacher.

The crowd mostly was New Yorkers dressed in semi-western clothes, but Friedman, as usual, brought out orthodox Jewish fans, many wearing yarmulkes.

The Long Star Cafe has become the place in New York to hear real live country-western music, from Friedman to Freddy Fender to Ray Wylie Hubbard. "This (the cafe) is an organic thing and after a while took on its own life force," explained Cooperman. "I go with what the people want."

They want Texas. However the Lone Star Cafe is defined, it fits Larry King's formula of "playing cowboy." It is not quite real, but it thrives on the unreality. Cooperman plans more live Texas music at his annual San Jacinto Day celebration, and very soon an art gallery featuring only Texas artists will open in the Lone Star Cafe's loft. On top of that, more is planned.

"In August," says Cooperman, "I think we'll get the guys from Luckenbach and maybe Ray Wylie Hubbard and block off 13th Street and do a rodeo."

And perhaps after that goathead stickers will sprout in New York streets, Mayor Koch will begin driving a pickup with a rifle rack in the back window, the 21 restaurant will feature chicken-fried steak, moon pies and R.C. Cola on its menu. All New York voices will twang like those from Monahans. Oil will be discovered in Central Park and the tree that grows in Brooklyn will be a mesquite.

There's no sense going half way with this Texas thing.

1979

THE FORT WORTH STRANGERS

In the beginning, the world of the Fort Worth Strangers was void, and without form, and possibly the worst idea I ever heard.

This is my dish of crow. I was wrong.

By any reasonable measurement the Fort Worth Strangers were a phenomenon. A national wonder. Perhaps no more than this season's hula hoop or Farrah Fawcett-Majors or Green Slime, but nonetheless a national phenomenon.

A plea for T-shirts from Notre Dame students, a call for Stranger daily box scores from Pennsylvania. Cheers from "a bunch of real swell fans over here in Pompano Beach, Fla." Checks for T-shirts and caps and *Star-Telegram* subscriptions (". . . for as long as the Strangers play") from Connecticut and Chicago and Alabama. Petitions to move the Strangers' franchise to Wilkes-Barre, Pa., New Orleans, Boston ("How close is Milo to 3,000 hits?") and Brooklyn, N.Y. A chuckle from Walter Cronkite at the close of his CBS nightly news show.

And long-distance telephone calls from the sports editor of a major American newspaper to ". . . find out what happened today with the Fort Worth Strangers."

What happened was that the Strangers got famous. Also infamous.

Not everyone loved the Strangers, who were, according to many callers, "trash," "bad taste" and "embarrassingly unfunny."

If it matters—and several readers have indicated that it does not—adventures of that fictional, mythical baseball team, the Fort Worth Strangers, have concluded in the *Star-Telegram*, a fact that will distress the team's supporters, gratify its detractors.

The Fort Worth Strangers are no more, but have passed into the mists of time and microfilm and tombs of our newspaper morgue.

No doubt, memories of the Strangers will remain around a long time. Other memories will fade, and I have visions of some guy rummaging through an old trunk in his attic, 50 years hence, disinterring a tattered, yellowed T-shirt emblazoned with "The Fort Worth Strangers" and wondering aloud, "Who the hell were they?"

They, sir, were a famous baseball team of September 1979.

It is far simpler, though, to explain who and what they were not, than who and what they were.

They were not real.

Not any of them, not the Runt; not Marvelous Feets, baseball's only left-handed second baseman; not Inca Inca Doo Zepeda, the Siamese twin Inca Indian; not Bones; not Jelly; not the big guy, Milo Candidi; and certainly not the limp-wristed, switch-hitting Stranger superstar shortstop, Larrupin' Lou, who will never be Anita Bryant's weekend house-guest.

None were real. They were fiction. Made up. Figments of my and many imaginations. They were not real; they were unreal.

Being unreal, the Fort Worth Strangers most of all were not the Texas Rangers.

The Fort Worth Strangers were neither a satire on, nor a parody of, the Texas Rangers.

Early on, we pledged to separate the teams, resolved to design each Stranger character so he would not in any way resemble a real Texas Ranger player. When writing strayed too closely to the Texas Rangers, an editor slashed away.

The Fort Worth Strangers, I repeat, were not the Texas Rangers.

That is the truth but few of the Stranger detractors will

believe the statement, and we, I suspect, are stuck with the libel.

The Strangers affected readers that way: Loved them or hated them, in about equal portions as nearly as we could determine, though there were others who took the sanest course and ignored the entire matter.

"What is it?" a caller asked soon after the Strangers appeared.

"Fiction," I replied. "The Strangers are a fictional baseball team playing fictional baseball in a fictional story."

"Oh, I see . . . but what is it?"

Well, to begin, the Strangers were not my idea, did not in fact fit my September game plan, which was a vacation.

The editors did it, dreamed up the Fort Worth Strangers, although the idea germinated in the pages of a master's degree thesis by Anne Tinsley, wife of Executive Editor Jack Tinsley.

She critiqued "The Universal Baseball Association Inc., J. Henry Waugh, Prop." by Robert Coover, a critically acclaimed but little-read book in which baseball is a metaphor for life. A cultured little tome about a fictional baseball league.

Enter David McHam, stage left. Acting head of the SMU Division of Journalism. An editorial consultant for the *Star-Telegram*. McHam read Ms. Tinsley's thesis. Time lapse. In mid-August, *Star-Telegram* editors and McHam "retreated" in East Texas (at the hamlet of New York in case historical markers ever are needed).

Editors, like managers of even Vegematic food-chopper factories, conduct periodic "retreats" from the routine of daily work life. That is the way of modern business. A "retreat" is a time in which new ideas are invented, old policies and procedures rehashed, the future mapped.

Sometime during that "retreat," in that piney woods burg near Athens, McHam, perhaps euphoric with fresh air, suggested the *Star-Telegram* create and publish a series about a fictional baseball team.

The idea was that the fictional baseball team would

be something with which some of the readers could have a little fun.

The retreating editors—Assistant Managing Editor Henry Holcomb, Metropolitan Editor Katie Sherrod, Public Affairs Editor Glenn Guzzo, Evening City Editor Lou Hudson —leapt on the idea.

The Fort Worth Strangers—a small fanfare might be in order here—had been conceived.

Back in Fort Worth, on the weekend of Aug. 18–19, Sherrod pedaled her bicycle to my home, and began selling fictional baseball.

No, sorry, I said. September's my vacation. No, got to do some work around the house. Sorry, my back's been acting up lately. No. Never. Absolutely not, it's a terrible idea, and the next morning I sat down at the typewriter and began inventing the Fort Worth Strangers.

The Strangers were introduced on Sunday, Sept. 9, in an "official program," and they were born with the uncanny, kismetic kiss of the best of timing and the worst of timing.

The worst of timing was that the Texas Rangers were on a losing streak and did not appear to be contenders for the American League West Division championship. Ranger fans were edgy.

The best of timing was that September, the dog days of summer, is a dead period in the news business, and life in general. The kids are back in school. Lingering heat is crumpling the spirit. Football has not yet reached its usual feverish, frenetic pitch. And the summer of '79 was not an auspicious time in history. Fuel shortages, long gas lines, high inflation rates, short tempers.

People perhaps were searching for something with which to ease their strained mood through the dog days, and along came the Fort Worth Strangers.

I wish I could report that we deliberately, purposefully set out to launch a September phenomenon. But we didn't. We wanted only to provide a light transition into autumn, and have a little fun.

The Strangers were serendipitous, an unexpected success.

Not, of course, in the beginning.

Hardcore baseball fans were furious, believing as they did—and possibly still do—that the Fort Worth Strangers were only a thinly disguised slur on the Texas Rangers.

"Childish." "Extremely poor taste." "Asinine." "Stupid." "An insult to the reader's intelligence." "The former great *Star-Telegram* sportswriters must cringe at this stupidity." "This is the most stupid junk I ever saw in a first-class newspaper."

If there is any solace for the Texas Rangers in all of this, it is that they have a rather large and vocal gang of supporters out there.

Those who telephoned were equally incensed, but their responses mostly are unprintable. An early caller angrily denounced me as "an atheist," charging that "Jesus said 'If you are not for me, you are against me' and you are against the Texas Rangers."

"The Lord," he added, perhaps implying that God reads baseball box scores before breakfast, "will punish you, the editor of the *Star-Telegram* and the newspaper."

One of the concessions made to me when the Strangers project began was if they were not being accepted by readers we would quickly end the series. I began looking through an atlas for a convenient mountain on which to crash the Strangers' team plane.

Other callers, not as angry, indicated that the Strangers were not really the kind of work a grown man should be doing, as if I had not been scribbling about hunchbacked batboys I could have been working on my speech before the United Nations.

There was another stripe of protest about the strangers, that from readers who saw the fictional baseball team as a blasphemy of the First Amendment, a heresy of journalism, and it did no good to point out to them that a daily newspaper is a whole of many parts and entertainment is a proper and common ingredient.

Already, I argued, there is a daily page of fiction in newspapers, including the *Star-Telegram*—the comics (and, it might be added, the astrological charts). Why should a clearly labeled piece of fiction about a baseball team create such a furor?

Serialized fiction in newspapers has a long and honorable history. Until the late 1930s most major newspapers regularly published fiction. Stir around in the *Star-Telegram* microfilm bins and you will uncover the corpses of dozens of serialized fictional adventure stories (Rex Beach—a personal friend of Amon Carter Sr., this newspaper's founder and long-time publisher—was a favorite author).

But in modern newspapers, admitted fiction has been missing for several decades, although in the past few years newspapers in San Francisco, Chicago and Philadelphia have created and published serialized soap operas.

The Strangers, we think, were unique.

Doubtless, they were outrageous and much of the early consternation must have been that they played at not a minor watchful team sport like, say, lacrosse, but The Great American Pastime, and not everyone believes it should be an object of satire. One of the problems of the Strangers is that I am not a baseball fan. I enjoyed playing baseball in high school and junior college and for a semi-pro Sunday league, but watching baseball, for me, is somewhat like watching the breeding of elephants—once the grandeur and spectacle of it all is absorbed, the rest is pretty commonplace and boring.

So blame for the extended parodying of baseball itself must be laid on me, and not the rabid baseball fans here in our office.

And that is a major point. The Strangers affected *Star-Telegram* staff members as it did the readers. "I thought you had more pride than to put your name on something like that," said one.

"I know it's dessert for the reader," challenged another, "but shouldn't we give them more meat and potatoes?"

For those readers critical of the entire Strangers' project, there are three persons who need to be absolved of any and all blame—*Star-Telegram* publisher Amon Carter Jr. (he is, coincidentally, a Texas Ranger minority stockholder), and our baseball writers, Bob Lindley and Jim Reeves. None had anything to do with the Strangers; none, in fact, even knew the Strangers were on their way.

The Strangers were entirely an invention and project of the *Star-Telegram* news department, not the sports department. Lindley and Reeves were forced to face the Texas Rangers, Texas Ranger front-office personnel (one of whom, in a national article, called the Strangers "high schoolish"), and probably worst of all, their peers, sportswriters from other newspapers.

"Nobody's said anything lately." Lindley admitted, glumly, as the Strangers season prepared to close.

Amon Carter Jr.—who told the *New York Times*, "I don't understand it and I don't like it"—surely shouldered more criticism than any of us in the editorial department, and he should not be blamed.

That is the way it was for almost a week.

Then, for reasons I still cannot understand nor adequately explain, the Fort Worth Strangers became famous.

Suddenly, there was an outpouring of support for the Strangers. A fan club was formed by TCU student Skipper Shook, and we were forced to print membership cards. The Strangers were the talk of saloons and bars around town. A college professor was using the series in his lectures on modern satire. Letters arrived from readers who were playing the Strangers' game, issuing instructions for the characters' behavior, planning the team's future (at last count, our mail in support of the Strangers was seven or eight times the number of critical letters).

Radio stations, specifically KVIL with Cat Simon and WFAA in Dallas, began giving their listeners daily progress reports on the Strangers.

Bill Weaver Sporting Goods advertised and began selling T-shirts and hats emblazoned with the Strangers' feisty little logo, sold in fact 300 shirts and 200 caps at five bucks each in little more than a week, and sold them everywhere, even to fans in Hawaii.

Joey Parton, who manages team sales for the sporting goods company, said he knew the Strangers were "going to catch on"—which was more than we knew—the moment he heard the firm's employees laughing over the first article.

"I knew that if we liked it," he said, "probably there would be a market out there."

Most buyers were women. The men were in their 20s and 30s.

The ordeal of buying T-shirts for a fictional sports team embarrassed some men, which created a situation at Bill Weaver's like this:

". . . uh . . . You got that Stranger stuff?"

"Yes."

". . . uh . . . I need a shirt . . . uh . . . for my kid. He's in the fourth grade and . . ."

"What size?"

". . . uh . . . extra-large."

One customer, apparently serious, asked at Bill Weaver's for directions to the Strangers' luxurious ballpark, Cowtown Stadium, which we fictionally situated on the large parcel of vacant land at South Hulen Drive and the Trinity River, across from the Cullen Davis mansion. The customer was given directions to Cowtown Stadium, and perhaps even drove there expecting to see a modern, multi-use sports facility complete with chocolate nacho-making machines and a Western Auto Store.

That was another problem. Some people believed the Strangers were real. Skipper Shook encountered a TCU coed who believed in the Strangers. An elderly lady baseball fan who telephoned me at home was incensed that the *Star-Telegram* was only now getting around to providing news coverage on "Fort Worth's own team."

There was another phenomenon of the Strangers. Dallas. There has never been a clamorous demand for the *Star-Telegram* in Dallas. The Strangers' radio coverage changed that. Stories about the team were daily mimeographed and passed about. In at least one federal office, adventures of the Strangers were read aloud daily.

All of that, and more, including, somewhere in town, a

new baby wearing diapers imprinted with the Fort Worth Strangers' logo.

And so the Strangers became famous but at this point they still were only a local phenomenon, still controllable.

Enter the national press.

On Monday, Sept. 17, the *New York Times* printed on the front page of its sports section a longish story about the Fort Worth Strangers. Suddenly, the Strangers had credibility and national respectability.

A day earlier United Press International had written a Strangers story and wired it to member newspapers. The *Philadelphia Inquirer* printed a lengthy story and shipped it down the Knight-Ridder news wires. The Associated Press prepared and distributed to its 1700 member newspapers a full explanation of the Adventures of the Fort Worth Strangers. And the *New York Times*' wire service customers received a complete rendition of those fictional Strangers.

The four major wire services saturated the American newspaper industry.

But more was coming for the Strangers. One morning—Tuesday, Sept. 18, I believe—there arrived a CBS camera crew and Eric Engberg, the network correspondent. Two evenings later, the Strangers closed out the CBS Evening News with Walter Cronkite before an estimated 16 million people.

Engberg and his crew had done the impossible. Television is a visual medium. It requires something to show the viewing audience, and how do you photograph a non-existent baseball team? Although I thought the camera lingered far too long on my bald spot, Engberg solved his problem by interviewing Leonard L. Leonard, the baseball immortal and Strangers' manager (portrayed by the impish C. L. Richhart).

There, before 16 million people, and dressed in his incongruous costume of aloha shirt, crumpled aviator's cap and what appeared to be a strand of cheap Woolworth beads, was Leonard L. Leonard in the flesh, contending that his team, the Fort Worth Strangers, indeed had a shot at the American League West Division of professional baseball. "And," cackled

Leonard, "If we don't have enough time, we'll just ask for an extension of the season."

That evening, the familiar voice of Walter Cronkite, whose weary job it is to inform us of wars and high crimes and disasters and all the sorrowing foibles of mankind, closed out his daily report to America with a discernible chuckle about a non-existent, ragtag collection of misfits— the Fort Worth Strangers.

From that moment on the Strangers took on a life of their own, were beyond control by me, by any of us. They had a life force. And we were compelled to change their destiny.

From the beginning we had no idea what would happen to the Strangers, what their fate would be two or three weeks hence. "Will they play for the World Series Championship?" a few early fans wanted to know. We had no idea. There was, however, a plan in the back of my mind to make them lose early thereby solving the World Series question and perhaps salvaging something of my lost vacation.

So I visited upon the Strangers a martyr's load of troubles, from exorcisms in the dugout to fan riots on the field. Somehow, the Strangers persevered and I was prepared to attack them with pestilence, plagues and famines—until they became famous.

With fame came new insight to the character of the Stranger players. Runt Rovinsky, in my mind a brattish, arrogant, foul-mouthed malcontent, became, well, cute. Doc Sisco, an intellectual snob, was wise and worldly. Gay as a grig though Larrupin' Lou may have been, his sexual preference became unimportant; he was a superstar, the best damned shortstop in baseball. And Milo. Hulking, menacing Milo, who ate bars of Irish Spring and chewed on dugout benches and shed hair all over Tandy Turf playing surfaces, became the most popular Stranger of them all, a giant teddy bear with a fierce determination to win.

Because the Strangers became somehow imbued with humanity, it would have been criminal to allow them to lose, so they won the American League West Division by soundly whipping the California Angels, 12-8, in a game recreated and broadcast by WFAA radio for what everyone suspects was a huge audience.

That evening, too, with former Dallas mayor and sportscaster Wes Wise doing the play-by-play and Joe Holstead, WFAA's program manager, handling the color, the Strangers became even more real, and I defy anyone who listened to claim he did not feel like cheering when Larrupin' Lou hit that game-winning grand slam home run.

It was Leonard L. Leonard, as embodied and personified by Richhart, who gave the Strangers a kind of lasting fame. Glenn Dromgoole, an assistant managing editor and the man charged with fitting the Stranger project puzzle together, had the inspiration to employ Richhart to portray the laid-back, existential, Yeng-fulfilled Leonard. The clench-fisted, toothy portrait of Richhart/Leonard, taken by *Star-Telegram* Chief Photographer Gene Gordon, is a kind of joyous celebration of life that long has been the real character of Richhart.

When word reached us that CBS television was on its way to the *Star-Telegram* it was decided that Richhart should be here to portray Leonard L. Leonard. Katie Sherrod telephoned. Rich can't come right now, she was told. He's sitting in a tree in the backyard. None of us found it odd that an octogenarian named C. L. Richhart was sitting in a tree. We would have been surprised had he not been there.

Other Strangers pictured were a collection of *Star-Telegram* employees and well-known Fort Worthers. Milo Candidi was played by another bear of a man, my friend, Associated Press correspondent and soon-to-be-published author of the quintessential book on the trials of Cullen Davis—Mike Cochran. Bob Ray Sanders, KERA radio's station manager and a *Star-Telegram* columnist, was Marvelous Feets Lisenbee. Bill Benge, a vice president of Jerre R. Todd & Associates, was Jelly Hartung. Jarrold Cabluck, a successful photographer, was Inca Inca Doo Zepeda. Little Boy Dittmar was played by attorney Kirk Purcell. Larrupin' Lou Merkle was Jan Hubbard, a *Star-Telegram* sports writer. Runt

Rovinsky, Bones Zygadio and Hod Dimaggio were played, respectively, by *Star-Telegram* copy editors Tommy Hughes, Pete Wyckoff and Bob Merriman. Dude Adami was Jim Jones, the newspaper's religion editor. Buster Flick was John Gandy of our sports department. Ossie Goslin was played by Mike Perry, the assistant business editor.

Colnette Dragich, a Braniff International flight attendant, was Gloria (Sic Transit) Zepeda Mundi Leonard, the first woman pitcher in professional baseball.

And Doc Sisco—that was the guy who started it all: David McHam.

Mike Blackman arrived at the *Star-Telegram* as the new special projects coordinator and it became his duty to juggle the Strangers daily stories, and sniff out and correct errors, of which there were many, mostly mine.

Public Affairs Editor Glenn Guzzo deserves a special niche in the Fort Worth Strangers' history. Quite simply, Guzzo is a baseball fanatic, and an expert. He is one of those guys who can tell you who batted .234 in the World Series of 1923, or who owns the record for most runs batted in by a left-handed hitter playing in his second year for a last-place team in 1952.

Guzzo also was the designer of the classic championship showdown game between the Strangers and the Angels.

When we decided to end the Strangers' season with WFAA's re-created game, Guzzo, the baseball purist, was incensed. "They haven't played a full season," he protested. That's why the Strangers were forced to play three doubleheaders in four days, to satisfy Guzzo's demands for a 162-game season, just like real baseball teams. Days after the Strangers series concluded in the *Star-Telegram*, Ed Brice, our popular reader advice columnist, received a letter from a lady.

"Please explain to me," she wrote, "who are the Fort Worth Strangers?"

They, ma'am, were a famous baseball team of September 1979.

1978
AFTER THE FACT

*On August 1, 1966, from the tower on the campus of the
University of Texas, Charles Whitman shot and killed sixteen
people and wounded thirty-one others during a ninety-four-
minute siege.*

In those days I had a secretary, two assistants and respectability. The last purely was honorific, varying from hour
to hour by whim of Joe Belden's private voter poll.

If Texas Attorney General Waggoner Carr (whom I served
as coolie-in-residence for his campaign to depose Senator
John Tower) fell a point or two in the public marketplace my
esteem as a flack drooped. Some days it collapsed entirely.
The problem was that the public liked Carr as attorney general; it did not care for him as senator. I, officially, was on
leave of absence from the *Star-Telegram*, serving six months.

My secretary was a bovine creature, addicted to cheese-
burgers, Cokes and false eyelashes. She had a genius for chewing gum, tapping her foot, typing and listening to hard rock
via ear plug. She had astonishing muscular coordination; jaw,
toe, finger and ear worked as a unit.

So it was August 1, 1966. Austin was a fog of wet summer heat. We headquartered in the old Sears building on
Congress Ave. (My desk was upstairs near the former plastic
refrigerator bowls counter.) 11:45 a.m. The secretary was
rigged up to her transistor.

"Hey," she said, "There's a guy on the tower shooting
people. He's killed five."

Fifteen minutes later a policeman blocking Guadalupe—
the drag bordering the University of Texas' western edge—allowed me through. Reverting to type, I had called the *Star-*

Telegram, talked with the city desk and gotten permission to "see what's going on."

A block from the campus I found a parking spot. It seems silly now but I actually paused to put a nickel in the meter, proving something or other about social conditioning. Spectators were everywhere, behind trees and buildings, crouching behind cars. It looked like those television news films of revolution in South America.

There is no reality in those situations. I played the game as the others, trotting in a stooped position from tree to bush, until I arrived at a building across from the UT tower. Others, perhaps a dozen, hid there. Above, I could see the tower. Small puffs of smoke. Airplane—a Piper Cub, I think—circling high above. Gun noises. Real rifle shots do not make movie sounds. They are blunt, flat without the drama of resounding zings or ricochets.

I went to the building's southeast corner. A policeman, rifle in hand, was crouched. It was there, I think, that the truth of what was happening became clear. The flat mall area was littered with bodies. Some moved, but hesitantly. Most made no movement.

I stayed behind the building for almost an hour and can remember little except the continuing gunfire. There was a remarkable conversation between a young girl and boy. They discussed their date that night, deciding to start at 7 p.m. Life goes on.

About 1:15 p.m. a hand was seen waving a piece of cloth from the tower. A radio broadcast said the sniper was dead. I ran around the building and into the tower's ground floor entrance. From everywhere people were converging on the tower. Inside, dozens of cops were organizing. I walked to the tower elevator. An ambulance attendant stood there, holding a stretcher. A police sergeant called to his men, "Block off the hall and elevator." I put a hand on the stretcher, the elevator doors opened and we went in. There were 10 of us. I was the only reporter.

I recall the elevator made a clicking sound, at five-second intervals, as we moved up 26 stories. No one talked, hardly breathed. When the door opened, a policeman clutched his pistol. In front of the door was the body of a young boy. A teenager, perhaps Latin-American. His eyes were closed. Right, up the stairs, another victim. A woman. Our feet splashed—literally—in her blood. The top, a reception room: A third body, a woman, stuffed behind the sofa.

Outside on the narrow walkway stood Officer Romero Martinez. He was in traumatic shock. He had shot the sniper, first with a pistol, then with a 12-gauge shotgun. Other cops cared for him.

To this day I remember every detail of Charles Joseph Whitman, as I saw him for the first time, how the concrete railing shadowed his right hand lying against his forehead, the slackness of his face posed in an expression of mild surprise, as though he could not believe Martinez was shooting him.

A doctor pronounced Whitman dead. Another officer removed Whitman's wallet and I copied his name, address, age and physical description from his driver's license. I took notes of what everyone said and did on the tower and never had an officer question my presence; I suspect the high tragedy numbed them as it did me.

Twenty minutes on the tower, and I left (having to crawl back to the reception room door because idiots with rifles on the ground still were firing at the tower). Below, the building was locked. Thousands of persons stood outside. I looked for a phone, turned into the first office I could find. It was the records department where I was able to determine Whitman definitely was a university student.

I called the *Star-Telegram*. It was shortly before 2:00 p.m. I spoke with the p.m. city desk, offering what I had, which was the sniper's name, his university status. No luck. Nobody wanted it because it would be necessary to chase it into print.

I called the Associated Press, offering the info to a voice. The voice didn't trust the tip so I gave up, took myself off the campus and to the S-T capitol bureau office.

You cannot experience such a story without seeing the

history of it. I wanted to write it, yet bureau chief Harley Pershing, who had been away at lunch when the story broke, offered to interview me as an eye-witness. I declined.

The next morning I got what every reporter wants—the front page. It should be noted that although the lead news story contained my byline, another S-T reporter actually wrote it—extremely well, too—from my notes and wire copy. The sidebar, though, was mine. It was an account of what I saw and heard on the tower. I must have attempted 20 leads before hitting on "Charles Joseph Whitman lay in the shadow of his last afternoon." From there, the story wrote itself.

In retrospect, luck and coincidence got me a story. Luck that I was close enough to be among the first into the tower, luck that a stretcher was near enough for me to touch, giving the impression that I was a medical person, not a reporter, luck that of all the offices in the tower I chose the records room to claim a phone. There was some little stupidity, too, for in my pocket all the time was an attorney general's staff pin which would have admitted me anywhere and allowed me to speak to anyone. I forgot about it.

For weeks afterward I dreamed of Whitman and his victims. That day killed my taste for violent stories and not even now would I willingly do it again. I have a shell, an un-shiny brass casing, two-and-a-half inches long, tapered and crimped, stained with black streaks at the end which held the lead. Across the shell base is printed "R-P6MMREM." There is a tiny depression where the firing pin struck.

It came from Whitman's 6mm bolt-action rifle. I picked up the shell on the observation deck, where it was scattered among a hundred shells. A cop watched and then picked up a shell for himself. From being participants in a piece of history, we had become souvenir hunters.

1968

A CHRISTMAS STORY

Roy has been dead a long time now and no one re-
members. He had no friends and probably no family. Roy was
not the kind of man about whom anyone would reminisce.
People in the small East Texas town said only of Roy that he
was "the most useless man in the county." I suppose he was.
Roy—his full name was Roy William Simpson—never held a
job or did anything that could be considered steady work.
His only pastime was drinking. He consumed whiskey and
cheap wine in awesome amounts if he could obtain either but
usually he could not. More often he drank after-shave lotion,
hair oil, various cooking extracts and other everyday, ordinary liquids no one but Roy considered alcoholic.

Roy existed by stealing. He stole vegetables from gar-
dens and nearby farms. He stole from old man Otis Adams'
egg farm, though he never took chickens which would have
made Otis angry enough to call the sheriff. He stole only eggs
and old man Adams would joke about Roy's thievery to the
men gathered at the filling station—"Roy can steal an egg before it's laid," he claimed. They would laugh uproariously at
the thieving antics of the county's most useless man.

Once, between vegetable seasons, Otis' chickens quit
laying for some reason, and Roy was forced to steal Mrs.
Truax's registered poodle. He apparently intended selling the
dog for money with which to buy his distilled liquors or va-
nilla extract. The sheriff caught him and returned the poodle
to Mrs. Truax. Roy was not arrested. He was never arrested
for his thefts. Townspeople in fact rarely complained of Roy's
stealing. Roy was just an irritating cross they bore, like mos-
quitoes in the spring or a faulty sewer system.

Somewhere in Roy's background was a term in prison, probably endured for theft of something more valuable than vegetables, eggs or poodles. He rarely spoke of his jail days but he told me prison was not oppressive except that he suffered from a lack of alcohol. He had worked for a time in the penitentiary's license plate shop and later transferred to the laundry where he washed sheets and stitched up rips in mattress ticking.

Aside from stealing, Roy's source of income was a sad and cruel game. He was the object of ridicule for local teenagers and filling station loafers. The kids would say to Roy, "Bet you a quarter you can't run up to the cafe and back in 30 seconds." Roy could not and he knew he could not but he always tried. The quarter was his for playing the fool. He would start off in a kind of shuffling trot, pumping his arms in awkward thythm, like a man going nowhere. The kids would laugh and point at Roy or run along-side taunting him.

The adult loafers were no less cruel. A loafer would say, "Roy, can you dance a jig? Betcha four bits you can't." Roy would try. Or he would pat his head and rub his stomach for a dime. The teen-agers and adults never seemed to tire of the sad sport. Perhaps it was their unconscious way of supporting a tired, frail, liquor-ruined old man.

Roy had no status in the small town except that of cooperating buffoon. He could not even claim the title of town drunk. That honor belonged to the local bootlegger who drank more than he sold. That sot, according to the townspeople, had a regular, albeit illegal, occupation; Roy was unemployed. The bootlegger got Roy's money when he had any. If not, Roy would knock politely at the rear of the general store and Mr. Ferris would hand out a bottle of extract. There was an unpopular bond between Roy and Mr. Ferris, and the storekeeper was criticized by the church people for giving Roy the alcoholic extracts. But Mr. Ferris took a drink now and then and he laughed off the complaints from the town's more sober citizens. He continued to pass bottles out the back door to Roy. Mr. Ferris liked the old man. One Christmas he gave Roy a plaid scarf and Roy wore it like a regal ascot tie under his faded jacket.

The cruel pranks brought Roy a couple of dollars a week. Twice a year he received an envelope with a $10 bill in it. Most people speculated the letters came from a son or daughter but no one knew for sure. At those times he bought bottles of whiskey or gin and stayed drunk for a week. It mostly was after the $10 bills arrived that Roy was drunk on Main Street and people would tsk-tsk and complain that he was the most useless man in the county.

Because Roy performed for the jokesters they thought him not quite bright and perhaps he was not. Only rarely did he contribute more than a word or two in a conversation. But Roy was clever enough to live by the community's charity without a streak of shame and that requires some intelligence.

Roy was a man of years when I saw him, perhaps 55 or 56. His exact age was impossible to determine because liquor and poor diet long before had wrinkled Roy's body until his 130 pounds seemed bound inside a smoked sausage sack. I remember his voice as something unreal, gravelly and hoarse and low-pitched, the scratchy sound of cheap whiskey. His eyes were the color of stained copper, like old pennies, and his nose was too large for his face. I never saw him when he was not wearing the same clothes. His wardrobe did not change, winter or summer. Roy wore dark green, dirty corduroy pants, once-brown shoes with thin heels, a bluish work shirt and an ancient Eisenhower army jacket. The scarf given him by Mr. Ferris, red and green scotch plaid, either hung straight under his jacket or crossed in the continental style.

The jacket's regular buttons had been lost or removed and Roy had replaced them with bright, yellow plastic buttons. The yellow buttons only made Roy seem more of a fool.

Roy slept for years on a dirty old rug in the tool shed behind the cotton gin. When the area's cotton crop declined and the gin was torn down he moved to an abandoned sharecropper's shack two miles south of town, on land owned by the bank. He boarded up windows and stuffed wadded newspapers into cracks. For a stove he used a rickety ice box lined with asbestos shingles. Roy took the rug, his only possession, and continued sleeping on it.

The September before the winter in which Roy died the communty suffered a tragedy. Tragedy is the soul of small communities because one man's misfortune becomes public property. Tragedy assumes a collective face and the sorrow is borne by all.

Margaret Lee was not a pretty child. She was five, perhaps six, with straight blonde hair, the color of cobwebs, and watery blue, almost icy, eyes. She was thin and her skin was sickly white. The only time I ever saw her she wore a little girl's print dress and carried a battered rag doll across the crook of her left arm. Margaret Lee and her mother lived a block south of the filling station in a three-room frame house. The mother was plain, too, and big-boned, a large woman with a worn face. She came from Austria and spoke English with a low-keyed accent. Margaret's father had met and married the woman while stationed in Europe as an Army corporal. He brought her home to America, to the small East Texas town. The child was four when her father burned to death in a gasoline truck accident on a lonely Kansas road. Mother and daughter lived on the little insurance money left by the father's death. The mother baked pies and cakes for additional income.

In September doctors confirmed Margaret Lee had leukemia. Unable to save the little girl's life they set about the tedious work of prolonging it. The mother almost was insane with grief and cried hysterically when neighbors came to visit. The community gathered itself to help Margaret Lee. Each church held special collections for the child. Baptists beat Methodists but Methodist women took turns driving Margaret Lee and her mother to the county seat hospital and that charity was said to have balanced the smaller monetary contribution. The Lions arranged for a bloodmobile to come one Saturday and park on the empty lot next to Mr. Ferris's store. Townspeople donated blood to the child.

One of the pranksters brought Roy to the line and said, "Betcha six bits they won't take your blood, Roy." Roy stood his turn but when doctors saw the bland eyes, the alcoholic sheen of Roy's skin and his dirty beard and smelled his unwashed body covered by the Army jacket with yellow plastic buttons, they sent him away. Roy collected his 75 cents and got drunk in the alley behind Mr. Ferris' store.

A month before Christmas, Margaret Lee let it be known she wanted to see her grandfather. The mother did not beg, but she asked if it would be possible to raise enough money to bring the Old World grandfather to the East Texas town to see the granddaughter he had never met and who soon would die. Again the churches took special collections. Mr. Ferris donated a day's receipts from his grocery store and even Old Man Adams contributed his egg money. Someone asked Roy for a $2 donation and the loafers laughed when he snorted and stamped away.

Margaret Lee became weaker. Her mother argued with doctors who wanted to hospitalize the girl. The mother asked to keep Margaret Lee home until the grandfather arrived. So the Methodist women continued their weekly drives to the county seat hospital for Margaret Lee's treatments. More than a week before Christmas the letter containing airfare and expense money was sent to the small Austrian village.

The next day Margaret Lee lost her rag doll.

The Methodist lady whose turn it was to drive Margaret Lee to the hospital thought the doll had been left in the waiting room. Perhaps it was, but the doll could not be found when they returned to search.

So began another round of contributions by the church women. Dozens of rag dolls were delivered to Margaret, some store-bought, some homemade. The child rejected each and every one of them. None, she cried, was her rag doll. Her father had given the doll to her. That was the difference, explained the mother. Margaret Lee, pale and nervous and weak, announced that Santa Claus would return the doll.

Christmas approached and the town prepared to make the holiday the happiest ever for the little girl. They bought most of the smaller toys in Mr. Ferris's store and made trips to the county seat for larger games and mechanical contraptions.

On Dec. 23, Roy received one of his $10-bill envelopes

and immediately bought a supply of whiskey and gin. He struck out across the blackland fields and no one ever saw him alive again.

Although she was cranky and whiny about loss of her doll, Margaret Lee's last Christmas was splendid. The tragedy brought the town together as nothing before. There was a momentary rush of concern when Margaret Lee had to be taken to the hospital for more blood on the day before Christmas. She returned and was put in bed. A Lions Club member volunteered his pickup truck and toys were collected from homes and delivered to Margaret Lee's house at 10:00 p.m. on Christmas Eve.

Before she slept that night she talked about the doll Santa would return to her and about the grandfather who was expected in a day or two.

Christmas morning there were rag dolls, dozens of them, but not her rag doll and she cried as she hopefully opened each package. The mother held the child to comfort her. The rest of the day she played listlessly with her new toys and the unwanted rag dolls as she lay in bed.

Late Christmas day the snow began, huge uncommon flakes for that season in East Texas. Margaret and her mother watched the snow from a front window and they talked about the grandfather. Snow had covered the ground and lay in drifts around the house as darkness came.

I never saw the grandfather but people said he was a small man with a gray mustache and spoke no English. The grandfather and Margaret Lee visited for a day. Then an ambulance came and took the child to the hospital. Snow stayed on the ground for two days before melting but the weather remained unseasonably cold early in January and snow came again, not as heavily, but the ground disappeared once more under the layer of white. Late in January two rabbit hunters found Roy's body.

Roy's body lay under a small oak tree in the center of a field midway between the town and his shack. An empty whiskey bottle was beside him. Animals had fed on Roy's body but the sheriff said there was no mistaking who it was. Roy had not worn his Army jacket or the plaid scarf but the corduroy pants were his, so the sheriff identified the body that way. Roy, the sheriff reasoned, had gone into the field with his whiskey and passed out. He had died from cold and exposure. People said Roy, in death, was as dumb and drunk as he was in life; he should never have gone into the freezing weather without his heavy clothes.

Roy was buried in the cemetery behind the Methodist church, off in a corner, with the county paying funeral expenses for its most useless citizen. Sober folks saw Roy's cold death as retribution for a wasted whiskey-filled life and no one seemed to care very much that he was gone.

Margaret Lee died in mid-January with her grandfather at her bedside. Her funeral brought out most of the town's population. Mr. Ferris closed his store and even the loafers left the filling station long enough to watch Margaret Lee buried on a cold winter day beneath a gray distant sky.

The mother sold the frame house, and she and the grandfather left the little town and returned to Austria.

Almost a month passed before I heard about Margaret's rag doll. Mr. Ferris said she had the doll when the ambulance came to take her to the hospital, and he thought it was the doll she had lost. Later, when he noticed it closely he knew and he asked the mother about it.

Christmas day, an hour after dark when the snow had stopped, the mother heard a noise on the front porch. She opened the door. The rag doll lay in the snow, next to the steps. The mother saw no one.

Margaret Lee, the mother said loved the doll on sight. It was a pitiful thing, ugly and poorly made, but Margaret Lee said if Santa could not find her doll he knew the kind of doll she wanted. She loved the doll and cuddled to her as she lay dying in the hospital.

Mr. Ferris recalled that the doll was much like the old one, ragged and worn and lumpy.

It had, he said, red and green scotch plaid skin and, for eyes, two bright yellow plastic buttons.